LET'S PLANET TOGETHER

PRESERVING OUR EARTH IN UNIQUE WAYS

BENJAMIN TAYLOR

A SPECIAL GIFT FOR MY READERS

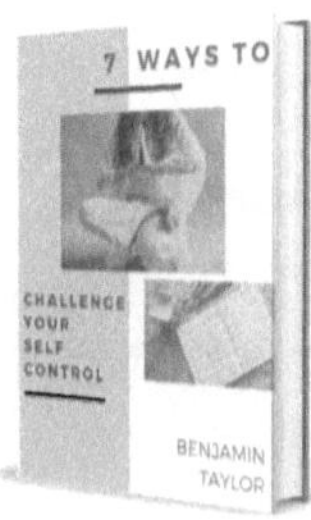

Included with your purchase of this book is our
Bonus Content,

7 Ways to Challenge Your Self-Control.

This booklet is a training for you to try with small day-to-day habits before you move on to making big changes in your life. These mini challenges can help you improve your health, and can help you save more money!

Click the link below and let us know which email address to deliver to
https://benjamintaylor.activehosted.com/f/1

INTRODUCTION

It was a Wednesday afternoon, and I woke up very excited. Wednesdays, you see, were the days when we were allowed to spend 20 minutes in the computer room. I would always play a mathematics game. I think. No, it was a puzzle game. Yes. What was it again? Uhm, Sudoku, yes! Well, Wednesdays were my Sudoku days! And as a very enthusiastic kid, who loved the environment, I made sure to remind the teachers to turn off their computers, devices, and all the lights when we were done for the day. Our teacher never minded because she was forgetful at times, especially when it came to such things, bless her heart.

But then something despicable happened! It was just after lunch, and I was walking back to class, talking to my friend. And that's when I saw it! Room C lit up with lights and not one but *five* computers that were still on and running games! Enraged, I stumbled to Mrs. NotToBeNamed's class. I went straight to my seat, crossing my arms and keeping my eyebrows furrowed deeply. I made it my mission to let her know that I was cross with her for not turning off those computers.

I gave her that note straight in her hands. I know it! Why would she ignore me? Does she ever read my reminder notes?

From there on, it was a very awkward language lesson. Whenever I was asked a question or called upon, I would simply respond with a personal environmental snark like, "Well, Mrs., I don't know. Is there a degree of comparison for ignoring one's letter and wasting energy?" Or maybe not something as specific as that. But I can guarantee you that the comeback was just as awful and weird! My poor teacher must have thought I was losing it at such a young age.

So, the day went by, with my ache still continuing. I didn't even enjoy my dinner that night, and we had burgers! It really bugged me! She would always thank me for leaving her those little reminders after I had noticed that she tended to forget about the electronics. So that night, I thought even harder about it while I was in the bath. And even more when I was dressed and tucked into bed. My mother had noticed, of course, but when I told her, she shrugged it off. But this was no laughing matter!

About 20 minutes in, I realized that no amount of sheep could soothe me to sleep. What was the point, really? I looked over to my right, where my blazer was huddled up on the floor. *There's a piece of candy in there. I just know it. There always is.* With a quick yet cautious peek at the open door, I decided to go for it! With short jagged shifts, I slithered off of my bed. *Just a bit further.* I cheered on, reaching with every inch of my fingertips out towards the fabric. *Got it!*

With a proud triumph, I pulled myself back in bed, a gleaming smile on my face as I searched around my pockets for the crunchy feel of the toffee wrapper. *Come on, where are you, you delicious risk? Aha, there you are!*

And then I pulled out what I thought was the toffee candy. But in a swift moment, my smile was gone. No, it wasn't candy at all. In my hands was a wrinkled piece of paper. I slowly unfolded the piece and as I did, broken letters started to flow together. *Wait a minute.* One more fold before everything had beat me like I was scrambled eggs. *That's my handwriting...*

We've all wanted someone to blame for the state of the world; it's our basic human nature. But the simple fact of it all is that there's not just a single person who should take the fall. We've all played our part in harming the environment, consciously or unconsciously, making decisions that either worsen or lessen our environmental scarring. Long ago, people were too occupied just living their lives. There were rare occasions where someone would glance over to see how the planet was holding up.

But then, there was a shift in the world, where the customary ways of thinking and acting were broken. Crowds of people, like a school of fish, were streaming towards helping our environment as they started to realize the tremendous damage that has stained our planet. Since then, it's been a revolution of green waves that would stop at nothing to wipe away all the pollution in the oceans, land, and sky.

The land hasn't fallen from underneath our feet, and it's because of people like you: the ones who are making a change or want to start doing so.

But where to start? Many environmental problems are smacking us in the face, so which one do we tackle first? The thing is, you see, some of us don't know how serious these problems actually are and how many threats are hidden.

I know that you want to understand these environmental problems so that you can give a helping hand, and in more ways than just recycling. I'm here to help because as that little boy with the reminder notes grew up, I also found myself lost in the busy world that was always just go, go, go. That is, until I learned to slow things down and stop for a moment and think about how my actions are hurting the biodiversity and richness around me … Or whether my actions were a band aid on those wounds.

We all know that the Earth is in jeopardy, yet many people prefer turning away, as if it's someone else's problem. The problem with this is, however, that we only have one planet. There's no Planet B. No matter how hard Elon Musk is trying, occupying another one is a distant future dream. But why would we want that when we have such a beautiful treasure to call home? And what if we do find another supportive habitat: won't history just repeat itself?

But, we're too late! you might think. No. We're not. Though the health of our environment seems to be deteriorating with each passing year, there's still hope! You're proof of this. If we commit to changing our habits and lifestyle to fit a greener, more sustainable one, we can still turn things around!

As you might have noticed, my passion for the environment and its beauty has been rooted in me since I was a young lad leaving notes for my teacher to remember to turn off the computers. And it has never changed. All I hope for now is to spread the same passion to others who are eager to look after Mother Earth as she has looked over us.

You have to understand that I'm not pointing any fingers. It's not about who did what or what mistakes we've made. Mistakes are mistakes; we live, and we learn from them. All I'm here to do is help you, guide you, and show you that there are so many ways to take off some of that weight the world carries around, to help you walk onto this path without doubt and a head full of questions about how you could do more to help the environment and encourage others to do the same as you.

Change isn't easy, I know. And might I add how brave you are for taking on such an enormous decision in your life. It honestly gives me the hope that the good in the world will always outweigh the bad.

I don't want you to walk this road alone, then come to a crossroads or obstacle where you have no idea what to do next. That's the worst thing that could happen, and I don't want that for you. I want you to finish this up with a clear understanding of everything you were uncertain about. I want you to wake up with a new outlook on your life, waste, savings, and giving it your all. It's about comprehending the ways that your actions, habits, decisions, and voice changes everything. And I know that you want that for yourself and the environment too. Why else would you have this book open, reading the introduction, deciding whether or not to continue with this read? You're on a search for the correct answers and solutions to help you understand what your part in all of this is, right?

Look, I'm not someone who has all the answers. I'm just someone with a lot of passion, love, and experience in this world who wants to share it.

I'm writing this as a witness statement of what's going on in the world: a testimony of how climate change and our wasteful, careless habits lead to the planet's suffering. The word needs to be spread and our voices need to be heard. I write this as a thank you note to all of those, including you, striving for a change in the world, for a better tomorrow where the apex-species work together to save our home. This is the only way we stand a chance: if the whole world flocks together to join the murmuration unfolding above our heads. It's time to look up at it before it's too late. Tell me, do you see it?

1

―――――

LET'S NOT HORSE AROUND

*W*hen you're out on a date, start talking about *global warming...*

IT'S A REAL ICEBREAKER

In its diversity and richness, the living world is unparalleled, a breathtaking wonder comprised of billions of individuals and millions of plants and animals. These lives, in a cycle, work together towards the sustainability of the whole. We're dependent upon this system, as the system is dependent upon its biodiversity. However, because of our carefree lifestyles and neglect, we have diminished this biodiversity we once had.

We, as humans, are infamous for making mistakes; it's the basic make-up of our DNA. We make mistakes, and then we move on, hopefully learning from them. It's the same for all species. For example, animals, especially young ones, will learn and discover what endangers them in the wild.

Mistakes shape a foundation of learning to adapt, develop, and progress.

However, *this* slip-up is not trivial: it's tragic. And it's unfolding across the globe, and for a long time was barely noticeable: this is the problem. We tend to acknowledge our mistakes after they happen. When the time comes where all the damage we have done becomes that visible, it's almost too late. Shortly, we will no longer be able to live in what we know as the natural world, a home that is dying.

There was an abandoned house on my childhood street, and I was always intrigued by it. Even though no one stayed or maintained the property, nature took its rightful place. The greenery crept into and stretched up the walls, and the floor was a sheet of moss. The reason I tell this is to note that all hope is not lost. I have faith in our ability to set our mistakes right. The time to act, however, is now.

THE PLASTIC PLANET

Right now, we're facing a manmade disaster of a global scale. Our greatest threat in thousands of years. If we don't take action, the collapse of our civilizations and the extinction of much of the natural world is on the horizon. But the longer we leave it, the more difficult it'll be to do something about it. And you could happily retire. But you now want to explain to us what peril we are in. Um... and, in a way, I wish I wasn't involved in this struggle. [chuckles] Because I wish the struggle wasn't there or necessary. But I've had unbelievable luck and good fortune. Um, and I certainly would feel very guilty... if I saw what the problems are and decided to ignore them. (United Nations Climate Change Conference, 2018)

Apart from other factors, such as habitat loss and diseases, there's another reason our land animals are edging closer to their extinction: hunting. We hunt them for all sorts of reasons: meat, ivory, medicinal products, or plainly as souvenirs.

The case stands. The wildlife population has declined immensely. The bitter fact of it all is that 99% of these endangered species face the same direct threat: human activity. Not only do these species inherently deserve to survive, but they're also essential to our biodiversity. Every single species has a part it plays in the functioning of our world, each one ensuring the survival of the next.

Herds of wildebeest, gazelles, and zebras in the Serengeti, for example, require an enormous amount of healthy grassland to function. Without this vast space, the herds will diminish, sending the entire ecosystem into a collapse. These herds keep the plains rich and productive by fertilizing the soil. Likewise, bees pollinate thousands of plants, ensuring the survival of these plants and those who depend on them.

In the past, animals were simply commodities, sources of oil and meat. They had no place to hide from us and no comprehension of what we were doing. But then, an awareness of what was happening in the world developed. Humans started fighting against poachers and the wrongful acts against species.

Let's face it: no one wants wildlife to disappear. And with the number of conservation efforts, so much is already being done! But is it enough? No, it's not. Saving individual species, or even groups of species, would not work. I can't stress this enough: our world is one giant, constant machine, and every gear, fuse, belt, and bearing is crucial. Still, with that said, any step, no matter how big or small, is a step taken, which, in itself, already helps.

The thing is, *we* will always be the dominant species. We have turned thoughts into inventions that have given us food, safety, and health. We are, in some sense of the word, unstoppable. We are a widespread society of almost 7.9 billion, living different lives away from other wildlife. By 2050, estimates expect us to number nearly 10 billion. It shows just how rapidly our population is growing. And honestly, overpopulation also affects various other parts. With our need for more, we take more. Think about it. We have so many demands, desires, and things we produce, and all of these things we strip and pull from our surroundings.

Forests cover approximately 30% of the planet, meaning that half of them are already gone, cleared. I'm going to be quite blunt about this: forests are one of the habitats that will be lost. Around the globe, deforestation is occurring at an alarming rate. It's due in large part to animal agriculture, mining, and drilling. We benefit from the timber. The land that's left we use, we grow crops, farm, or build skyscrapers.

Plantations of palm oil (a common ingredient in processed foods, soaps, and cleaning products) hop up, leaving behind a habitat that's ultimately dead. Borneo is proof of it. The rainforests there were alive with life, hundreds of species of trees in a single block, and more than half of the land species lived there; among them were the orangutans. Orangutans spend years with their mothers, learning which fruits are worth eating. The training allows them to disperse seeds, and without this, numerous species of trees would fall. And what is a rainforest without trees?

And now, Borneo has nothing but regimented rows of palm oil, and the population of orangutans has reduced severely.

And it's not just the primates that are at risk and suffering: all of life is affected.

But, natural forests aren't just habitats and biodiversity reserves; they're also carbon sponges, soaking up the carbon and keeping it away from the atmosphere and oceans (also called 'carbon sinks').

This brings me to our next crisis: the very vast and blue habitat that's taking a much larger hit than you would expect.

Let's start with the fishing industry. Large fishing fleets would sail out, pulling from the waters large nets filled with fish. In the 1950s, there were plenty of fish to go around, but within a few years, they grew empty, with nearly 90% of the larger fishes already removed (Netflix, 2019).

When reeling in these fishes and other marine predators, the oceanic nutrient cycle, where nutrients are recycled continuously, would surely sink or disappear. Maintaining the industry was fundamental, so countries began to subsidize the fleets.

But, there were other parts of the ocean that were, and still are, dying. It's a tragedy that, at first glance, might even seem beautiful to the naked, unknowing eye: coral as white as snow. In truth, these are headstones in an underwater cemetery, the skeletal remains of dying life. Ocean acidification, overfishing, physical destruction, and human pollution bleach and burn these coral forests that were once vibrant.

Scientists discovered that climate change was extensively responsible for these bleached coral reefs. The ocean is warming, and we've been warned of this for some time now. Yet, here's more proof that our planet is heating up due to our lavish release of carbon dioxide and other greenhouse gasses. It might have seemed like the impacts were a distant problem, but they're not: the ocean was simply masking our damage, absorbing all our emissions. The effects are appearing right now, visible everywhere.

Contrary to popular belief, you should know that climate change and global warming aren't the same things. Global warming is a subcategory. Deforestation, extreme weather fluctuations, rising seas, the shift of wildlife populations and habitats: all of these are, among other things, collusion-aftermath.

The average global temperature continues to rise, and our planet is losing its ice. The most pristine of ecosystems is withering away, and with it, all life in the icy north and south.

Our air is polluted. I mean, imagine for a minute you've sealed yourself up in a room. A paraffin heater is on or a car is revving. Clouds of harsh smoke fill up the space. Breathing would hurt, wouldn't it? It would be hard, painful, and not to mention extremely dangerous. But then again, we've been doing this all along, haven't we? The room is just a very spacious one; it would surely be harder to notice.

Mountains are now made from plastic, tins, and straws as our trash problem only rises. The soil is degrading, falling apart beneath our feet. By damming, polluting, and over-extracting rivers and lakes, we've reduced the size of freshwater populations by 80%, we've overfished fish to critical levels. And quite frankly, I would be scared to drink some of the water even after it's 'purified.' And this was only air, water, and land pollution alone. There's also noise, sound, and thermal pollution all around.

We cut down 15 million trees annually, and the fertile land that's left we use for farming. We account for over one-third of the weight of mammals on earth, 60% of mammals we raise to eat. The rest we leave.

We're running out of resources and necessities. Freshwater takes up about 3% of the world. The other day, I read an article that explained and stressed how severe our water shortage had gotten. But little has changed so far—I'm crossing my fingers, though.

We can't cut down trees forever or artificially create berries, fresh air, or ice caps. And anything that we can't do forever, or will ultimately run out, is by definition *unsustainable*. If our population proceeds to grow as rapidly and we ravage as we do, there won't be enough to go around. It will all run dry. And we could end up chewing our way to the world's demise.

In David Attenborough's 2020 documentary, *A Life on Our Planet*, he shared foresight of what the future could look like; it's a wake-up call.

- In 2030, predictions paint a picture of the Amazon degraded into a savannah due to deforestation and lack of moisture. Species would be lost, the global water cycle altered. Arctic summers would be ice-free, meaning that the reflection of the sun's energy into space would sink. The pace of global warming will intensify greatly!
- In the 2040s, the north's frozen soils thaw, releasing methane. It's a pollutant emitted from oceans and the digestive means of termites and cows, among other things. Remember how cows farting was called 'harmful'? Well, it may sound humorous but it's

anything but. Methane is an instigator, an enabler of air pollution, a greenhouse gas that's even more potent than carbon. Climate change will accelerate!

- By the 2080s, soils will become exhausted by overuse, and global food production enters a crisis. Pollinating insects, such as bees, ants, and moths, will disappear. The weather's unpredictability will progress, natural disasters will come and go without warning, and seasons will interchange.
- Then in the 2100s, the planet would heat up, and large chunks of the earth would become uninhabitable, leaving millions without homes. The stability of our geological epoch, the Holocene, will be lost.
- The time for change will no longer be a possibility, and mass extinction will be underway.

We will become another chapter following the dinosaurs. That's if there will even be anyone left to remember our time, let alone write or read about it.

I would need years to list and explain everything that contributes to these problems or the possible outcomes, but we don't have the time. I think it's essential to get to where we want to be for us to see the efforts, contributions, and ways we all could do our part in changing the course we're on. If we don't, the future ahead is nothing but darkness, doom, and gloom.

But first, I would like to say a few last words before we move on. Although everything so far has been frightening and, frankly, depressing, you should focus on the crucial fact and takeaway of the chapter: *It's not too late*. We have the capability to restore stability to our planet and its biodiversity.

It all seems like such a great, vast space, regenerating itself constantly. The grasslands, forests, rainforests, and ocean all come together very purposely. But, it's all finite. How is it possible that everything we know will, someday, just disappear, run out? It's an arduous thought to comprehend. Yet, the reality is as simple as that. Our environment is limited, and we're ultimately bound by and reliant upon it. But still, as consumers, we devour the earth, depleting most of its resources and befouling the rest.

This is a human planet now; we rule it as if we're the only ones that matter, but nature will surely prove us wrong. Let's go back to that abandoned house from when I was a child: even when there were no people around, nature continued, unphased by the lack of activity. It moved around the evidence of anyone ever being there, rebuilding itself as it had done before. If we were to destroy our civilizations and environment, nature would continue without us. So, there will be a new world, with new species and those who survived the mass extinction. But we don't want that; we should learn to appreciate the power of nature and all that it's provided for us, or else, we will be forgotten.

Don't get me wrong. I'm not writing this to blame anyone. I myself am guilty of the state of our world. This is the truth. Some people are reckless with their actions, living a life that is too focused on their own problems to notice what has been going on around them. But as history will show, as people gain awareness of the natural world, they come to care for it. And you reading this is proof of just that, that the world still has a chance, because there are those who care about the planet and those living in it. So, let's stand together, not as individuals, but as a team working together for tomorrow and make this planet prettier than before.

MAKE LOVE, NOT EMISSIONS

I know it's hard to move on from that pressing conversation about the problems, but let's start over and focus on the solutions with a light-heartedness in mind, shall we?

Though the problems seemed like a heavy weight, the solutions are just as plentiful. It's important to recognize these solutions, even when we can't implement all of them, because only then will you fully understand everything that's going on in the world.

Crowd Control

Slowing down population growth is possible. There are signs globally of populations in certain areas, like Japan, stabilizing and hardly changing. As nations developed in the past, people chose to have fewer children. Think about it: in 1850, having six to nine kids was perfectly normal, while the average household now includes two to three children.

But the human population will peak someday. If we were to make it peak sooner and at a lower level, we could make it easier to do everything we have to. The trick to implementing crowd control would be to raise the standard of living worldwide: to pull people out of poverty, give them access to healthcare, and motivate children, especially young girls, to stay in school as long as possible.

Not only will it be an environmental benefit, but why not give people a fighting chance at a better life, with bolder opportunities and cheering support? We're all aiming to make the world a better place, after all.

Doing this might seem impossible at first. However, there are ways for this to happen. Economist, Geoff Riley, opined that living standards improve when an economy can sustain a rise in real per capita incomes and when the growth is widely spread. Basically, living standards will improve when an economy can handle and support everyone, rich and poor, getting more cha-ching!

A few ways for this to happen is to:

- Improve human capital
- Implement incentives to increase employment
- Create more and better jobs
- Boost social security
- Widen the accessibility to high-quality public services
- Implement good fiscal policies
- Increase minimum wage

And apart from these, there are many other ways to increase the quality of how we're living. However, most aren't in the position to make these changes or decisions. We can't boost the economy overnight, or make enormous, valuable contributions.

But, and I say this at the risk of sounding like a broken record, this is just an overview of possible solutions, and I want you to keep that in mind. Don't try to put every change on your shoulders. As we go on, you'll understand how you, as an individual, come into the mix, and how important you are in the ultimate solution. Just bear with me.

Wind Energy? I'm a Big Fan!

Imagine a world where we run purely on the agelessness of nature: sunlight, wind, and water. A renewable future where we phase out fossil fuel would be mind-blowing to witness!

We live in a world where every time a light switch is flicked, our need for more energy and electricity spikes. But, here's the perfect solution: the earth captures about 3 trillion kilowatt-hours of solar energy daily; that's more than enough! Not to mention how clean, quiet, and eco-tastic our cities would be. Renewable energy is highly advantageous and affordable. And it's just what we need: a power source that never runs out, because it's *renewable*.

We will no longer be dependent on imported fuels due to the diversity in our energy supply: I'm talking, economic development, jobs in manufacturing, installation, and more. Ultimately, the way of life will progress, pollution such as air and noise will reduce, and the environment will have a day off to recuperate.

Some renewable power technologies include:

- Solar (solar thermal for heat, photovoltaic for electricity)
- Wind (turbines, like those plastic windmill toys)
- Geothermal (the earth's heat)
- Biomass (plant and animal materials, even garbage)
- Hydropower (natural flow of water)
- Emerging technologies: wave and tidal power (same concept of hydropower, but with the ocean)

Generating energy on-site, like using heat pumps at state buildings, might be a good way for local governments to set an example, as well. They could also purchase green power or renewable energy sources. Combining these sources is a foolproof plan for the government to meet its goals.

Yes, obstacles are there. But the possible technical, financial, and regulatory problems are only hurdles. And with clear strategies and concrete steps, such as assessing potential funding sources and incentives, these barriers are easy to hop over.

Ironically, we're investing in fossil fuels, the very thing risking the future we're saving for. So why not swing for the fences and invest in renewables instead? And yes, at first, it might seem like a hassle, but in the long run, it'll be a home run for us!

'Seas' The Day

The simple fact is that our world can't function or revive itself without the ocean. As we know, the deep blue absorbs our carbon, which we should reduce, but we should also ensure that it's healthier and more diverse. This way, it will be able to offset even more carbon dioxide.

And by looking after marine habitats, more fish would start popping up on the radar. Let the fishing commence! This vast habitat will always be a valuable bowl for most of us, and if we do it right, the sea could turn back into a wilderness where we could all live and get along. It's a win–win!

Palau, a Pacific Island in Oceania, is proof. They're a nation reliant on their coral reefs for fish and tourism, it's their bread and butter. So, when their bread dwindled, they restricted fishing practices and even banned them from many areas. Then, something astounding happened: populations of protected fish were healthier, and soon they were spilling over into the areas open for fishing. The local fishermen saw that their catches were building up! And it was the work of the *no-fish zones*, which also allowed coral reefs to recover. What if we were to follow Palau's example worldwide?

Estimates imply that no-fish zones would be sufficient in providing us with all the fish we would ever need while ensuring the protection of extant species. In international waters, efforts are already there, with the United Nations striving to put up the largest no-fish zone of all.

Furthermore, dumping, polluting, and mistreating our water has to stop, for the health of both the marine life below and the land above. The same goes for our freshwater. We should focus on educating others to motivate behavioral changes regarding consumption and lifestyles, from individual use to the use of water in supply chains of major companies.

And innovation is needed! With scarcity staring us in the face, we need to develop water conservation technologies, recycle wastewater, improve irrigation, agriculture practices, water catchment, and harvesting. We need to be doing more to save water, and this is the leading truth: we should think before we drink, and save every drop!

I'm Rooting for You

The conservation of wildlife should be one of our top priorities. We've got to look after our animals, by preserving and restoring habitats and protecting them against threats, such as poaching and wildlife trade. Apart from protecting our marine life, we should also take into consideration what we could do for our land species, apart from scaring off poachers and dropping protected areas.

We should be reducing the stretches of land we use for farming so that there's space for the wild to return to. The best and swiftest way to achieve this would be to change our diets to plant-based. I know, a lot of you were sitting with your upper lip pulled up to your wrinkled nose! But, let's face it, larger carnivores are rare because there just isn't enough to sustain billions of meat-eaters; it's impossible. Maybe later we could try asking a lion to cut back on those gazelles, but for now, *we're* all we got!

By accepting such a diet, we would cut back on half of the land we use, considering there would no longer be a need for ranches and all that. And with the commitment to raising plants, we would be increasing the yield of the land, restoring fertile soil, and allowing nature to get back on its feet.

We have to get back the land we need, and we can apply both low-tech and hi-tech solutions to produce more food from much less ground. We could, for example, move production to newer spaces, like indoors or smaller gardens.

Another farming alternative that's been the talk of the town for awhile now, is vertical farming: a practice that involves stacking crops in vertical layers that often incorporate controlled-environment agriculture and soil-less farming techniques to enhance plant growth.

One of the most acclaimed vertical farming companies out there is *AeroFarms*. Since their launch in 2004, they've changed the game with their aeroponic tech, that soilless farming I was talking about. Their techniques provide them with higher levels of precision and productivity with little environmental impact and minor risks. This indoor farming company, based in New Jersey, claimed its methods use 95% less water than conventional arable farming. And there are many companies—and countries—who have taken on vertical farming. Now all we have to do is take it inside, and leave the land for nature to tend to.

This brings me to another concerning matter: bringing back our trees. We must stop deforestation everywhere, immediately! Forests are fundamental in our planet's recovery, so this is a very important step that has to be taken. Oil palm and soya crops should be grown on land that was deforested long ago; after all, as we saw, there's plenty of it. But, don't get me wrong, not all of it, because we could do better than this.

A century ago, more than three-quarters of Costa Rica was covered with forest. By the 1980s, forests were reduced to a quarter of the country due to logging, where trees are felled and the timber is cut up and prepared. The government decided to act, offering grants for the replanting of native trees. In just 25 years, the forests returned once again. Imagine this happening across the world.

The return of the trees would absorb as much as two-thirds of the carbon emissions that have been pumped into the atmosphere. And why not have more green around?

In 1854, Chief Seattle said, "We do not inherit the earth from our ancestors, we borrow it from our children" (de Souza, 2020).

We are a species that constantly thinks about the future, thinking about what we'll be doing tomorrow and what the future holds for us. Now we know the possible outcomes: either a deserted world we let down or another that's harmonious. We still have the opportunity to restore this world to where it once was and to continue living in a home that's so incredibly beautiful.

2

THE ECO-SUPPORT MACHINES

I used to work at a recycling plant, crushing cans. But I had to quit because ...

IT WAS SODA-PRESSING

Leaders play a prominent role in changing the world's current environmental condition. They not only have the benefit of encouraging and influencing others to live more sustainably and implement more eco-friendly habits and changes into their own lives, but they also have the authority to carry out some of the necessary changes needed.

When a nation looks after the environment, their actions will spread to other neighboring countries worldwide. A ripple effect, if you must, will occur. This can be seen all over the world. Many countries are working toward the prosperity of a better tomorrow because, as the world grew aware of the dire situation of the planet, leaders and their people from various countries stood up to take action.

THE LAW WON

Around the world, specialized environmental courts have been stationed to combat human-caused destruction. There are over 1,200 of these systems, to date, in about 44 countries, operating on all continents except Antarctica. The boom in environmental courts is driven by an understanding of human rights and environmental law and how these rights overlap and work with each other.

An awareness of these plights, like the risks of climate change, started to grow. And with it, dissatisfaction with the general court system. Don't get me wrong: to some degree, it's understandable. The highest murder rate in the world is 83 per 100,000 inhabitants in El Salvador; with a population of 6.5 million, that's about 5,400 homicides (Statista Research Department, 2021). So, reasonably, they'll be more focused on reducing the number of murders they have rather than who doesn't pick up their litter. Courts do have to prioritize other crimes, and, sadly, they don't always feel like they've got the time to jump up at environmental injustices.

But, the problem is, these aren't problems you could simply shake off. Take India, for example. Their environment and public health have fallen noxious due to their intense air and water contamination. The thing is, their court system is notably slow, while the problems are very urgent! It's not a case where you can drag it on for over 10 years. Action is needed! And this is why we can't always rely on the general justice systems, even when they're not at fault.

However, the pressure from climate change and concepts like sustainable development was strong enough to create environmental courts that could focus on this alone. With a range of responsibilities, these courts aim to make decisions promptly, with all fairness in mind, while offering cheaper alternatives than your regular court system.

And they've worked like a charm! Take Peru as an example. They first established a specialized court around 2019 to deal with environmental violations, such as illegal mining, deforestation, and illicit trade in wildlife, mining equipment, and hazardous waste. Shy of a year later, the court already had nearly 3,000 complaints on their docket.

Another success story would be Australia's Land and Environment Court, which combats climate change and protects coastlines and national parks. They have been strongly operational since 1980, their longevity allowing them to evolve and experiment with different approaches. They're considered to be one of the most innovative environmental court systems out there. And according to them, the key to such a court's success lies in strong leadership, steady funding, political support, comprehensive jurisdiction, stakeholder overview, and of course, a passion for what they're fighting for.

But, nothing is perfect. Some experts even state that these courts aren't doing as promised, questioning their principles and saying that they're simply a band-aid for a larger problem of a weak justice system (Brigida, 2018). Yes, these systems have their blemishes. Some lack the resources and capabilities to follow up on cases, and in some, judgments are dropped.

But, accurately judging the value of the environmental court systems is not as easy. Laws governing the environment are constantly shifting, and climate change presents new challenges at every turn.

A one-size-fits-all approach is not how environmental courts work. And these courts have proven effective in many countries, like India. They're a line of defense, crucial in battling these eco-threats. Look, everyone is entitled to their own opinion, but for me, the implementation of these systems symbolizes the will of countries, leaders, and communities wanting to make a change and leave the living world behind, polished.

The Un-Slicked Laws

Noticeable, day-to-day dilemmas, like pollution and plastic, are the new way to go about environmental laws. And these laws are crucial in their goals. The world is indented with change, an awareness of these problems is raised, and communities are moved to action.

- *France: Cleaner streets and metal eats.*
- France has not only been getting tough on vehicle emissions by raising tax for high-polluting cars, like SUVs, they've also banned a range of single-use plastic items. So, say *au revoir* to paper plates, cups, and cotton buds! And they're not stopping there, with plastic cutlery, straws, styrofoam cups and containers, drink stirrers, and confetti next on their chopping block!
- *Thailand: Free from the terrible threes.*
- Thailand has slashed three types of plastics, microbeads, cap seals, and oxo-degradable plastics like some plastic bottles, from being used. And in a country where nearly 2 million tons of plastic waste is produced from plastic bags alone, they knew they had to do something. So, they leaped to join retailers, like department stores, to stop the use and giveaway of plastic bags in their shops.

- *United States: The ban on bags.*
- More plastic bags are getting dumped from the dumps, with the United States joining in. Albuquerque, New Mexico, only allows plastic bags thicker than 0.09 inches but, as you can imagine, paper and fabric alternatives are favored. The state of Oregon also hopped in by barring single-use checkout bags in retail stores and restaurants. And lastly, the city that never sleeps, New York, has put to sleep most types of single-use plastic bags and further launched the 'Bring Your Own Bag NY' campaign to urge shoppers to bring their own kits along on errands.
- *Palau: Putting the cap on sunscreen.*
- And we're back to the tiny Pacific nation of Palau. As we know, it's a place bursting with marine life, with thousands of species of fish and hundreds of coral reefs. They were triumphant with their use of the no-fish zones, but when they were hit with coral bleaching, they were quick to step up to the plate once again. In a set of protective measures, all kinds of sunscreens were put in the shade. But why ban it? According to the US National Oceanic and Atmospheric Administration, it's because of the ingredient in sunscreen responsible for absorbing UV light, Oxybenzone, which could harm marine life, leaving coral reefs bleached and vulnerable to climate change.

So, a quick word of advice would be to know your environmental laws and to stick to them, and to think before you harm the environment, or else you could be seen in court!

DECLUTTERING THE DUMP

With the world generating 2.22 billion tons of waste annually, it's easy to see why we're in a trash crisis. And to make matters worse, at least 33% of this waste, according to The World Bank, isn't managed in an environmentally safe way (World Bank, n.d.). It's a mess. I saw a painting the other day of a young girl swimming in an ocean filled with plastic, rubbish, and scraps. Is this what we want for the future? Luckily, most would answer no. And, thankfully, efforts are being made to bag up the waste!

Wise Ways to Manage Waste

Waste management is critical to creating sustainable and livable cities, yet it's still a challenge in many areas mainly because it's a costly service that requires an efficient, sustainable, and socially supported approach. So yes, some things should be tweaked. Creating new landfills isn't enough, and conventional waste-management methods and incentives are, in some ways, failing us. That's why we should be turning our attention and taking notes from the most innovative waste control solutions worldwide.

- *Columbia: Rewarding-recycling.*
- Columbia generates a lot of waste. So, to overcome this problem, they came up with ECOBOT, a recycling initiative that pushed people to recycle by actually incentivizing and rewarding citizens for every recycled item. It's a machine that works quite simply, a sort of reversed-vending machine in malls, institutions, and public spaces to better boost recycling. So, how does it work? Let's say you have a bottle and its caps: you deposit the items, and then in

return, you get a coupon from associated companies or Eco partners, like restaurants and theaters. And that's that: the collected items are then sent off to recycling plants.

- *Indonesia: Wholesome waste.*
- Waste was piling up, and with Malang's majority without health insurance, their welfare was dwindling. That's when Dr. Gamala Albinsaid, a healthcare entrepreneur and CEO of Indonesia Medika, saw a window of opportunity. He created Garbage Clinical Insurance, which is just as it sounds: garbage for medical services and medicine. People, especially those of low-income households, are inspired to recycle their trash to finance their health. The clinic then sells the rubbish to recyclers, and the money is spent on giving people basic health insurance. It's a system that tackles not only waste but poverty as well. I mean, what a way to fill two needs with one deed!
- *Sweden: Spare some scraps.*
- I know it sounds insane, but Sweden has run out of trash! Yes, they're even asking other countries for their garbage so they could keep their recycling plants running: recycling plants that produce heat for households and electricity for private houses. They've adopted an efficient recycling policy where less than 1% of their rubbish ends up in landfills, while the rest is recycled, heating up homes on those cold winter days.
- *Uganda: Plastic parks.*
- Another man who has used rubbish for the good of others is the artist and environmentalist Ruganzu Bruno. Bruno first started collecting the villager's

waste, then, with their help, he constructed swings and life-size board games for the children living in the slums of Kampala to enjoy. But, the amusement park was like no other, made entirely out of waste! Today, Bruno aims to set up 100 similar amusement parks in other parts of Uganda. What a way to recycle!

- *Semakau Landfill: Rubbish island.*
- Singapore's first and only remaining landfill, Semakau, isn't your usual landfill. Instead of overflowing with trash, it's a place flourishing with mangroves, coral reefs, marine life, and birds. It's an authentic biodiversity hotspot that stuns away the usual image of your everyday rubbish dumps.
- *Germany: Bins are business.*
- Germany has really taken the environmental community by storm, aiming to better their eco-status by the day. They've cut off 49,700 landfills, the remaining dumping sites not accepting unsorted garbage and having a more sophisticated system handling them. They're also aiming to replace these landfills with plants, using them, as Sweden does, to produce energy. German entrepreneurs see waste management as a business that will someday lead the economy! This way of thinking shaped their innovative recycling system that has been replicated in many forms in several countries. It's called the green dot system, where manufacturers and retailers pay to get a green dot smacked onto the packaging of their products. The more packaging used, the higher the fees are, prompting businesses to reduce their packaging and recycle. This means less paper, thinner glass, less metal, and an overall decline of waste!

THE RECYCLING LEADERBOARDS

Now, first of all, don't let the heading fool you, this isn't a race or a match. Everyone recycling, or simply picking up that wrapper on the streets is a winner, but it's good to know that countries are pushing the hours to make the world a better place. So, let's get to it! Based on their recycling rates, according to Zuckerman (2021), the top 15 recyclers are:

1. Germany - 66.1%
2. Singapore - 60.6%
3. Wales - 60%
4. South Korea - 59%
5. Austria - 55.9%
6. Taiwan - 55.2%
7. Slovenia - 53.9%
8. Belgium - 53.5%
9. Switzerland - 52.7%
10. The Netherlands - 51.8%
11. Luxembourg -48.3%
12. Sweden - 48.1%
13. Denmark - 46.3%
14. Scotland - 44.2%
15. Italy- 43.6%

THERE ARE GREENER WAYS

There are honestly many people stepping up to help the environment, from recycling, waste management, laws, combating climate change, you name it! There's so much going into revamping the environment that we all should take a page from a few books around the world and apply it to our own lives as much as we can.

Greener travel, recycling, and green practices are present and applauded worldwide, with numerous community-led conservation efforts and get-togethers, as well as educational programs, striving towards the same goal: saving our planet!

3

JOIN THE GREEN SIDE

Why did the leaf go to the doctor?

IT WAS FEELING GREEN

Across the globe, people are becoming more aware of what they're doing, how they're living, and how they could be greener. But why is it important that we do this? Going green is a choice you make to contribute towards the betterment of the planet by coming up with new sustainable ways to help the earth and preserve it for future generations.

Evident by previous chapters, our environment is in a state of emergency. Every person has to do their part. And I know what you're thinking. What difference can one person make? Well, a tremendous one!

With nearly 8 billion people, one person can mean the difference between triumph or defeat. When every person plays a part, no matter how small, soon we'll have a giant working continuously to ensure the prosperity of our planet. If, for example, each person were to plant a sapling, soon we would have a forest! The power comes in collaboration, cooperation, and rallying to put things right.

Going green is a choice you can only make for yourself. To some, it might seem like an effortless pick. But not everyone is sure why that is. Going green has an ocean of benefits, and both you and the planet could reap in its rewards. And when looking at those benefits and all the outcomes of going green, it's easy to understand why.

But if the benefits I already gave you weren't enough, I'm more than ready to pitch it some more!

CLOSING THE DEAL

Going green is often misunderstood. It's not just something you do for the environment alone. Going green is also something you have to do for yourself and the ones you love. It's highly beneficial, leaving you feeling better and your wallet fuller. That's right, going green will actually be saving you money, and it's really not an expensive gig.

Are you thinking about putting the old house on the market? Well, a quick word of advice: make it eco-friendly! Doing so has been shown to boost the value of your home significantly. So, install those solar panels and invest in that water-saving toilet while you're at it!

And if you're not selling, or you just moved in, do these improvements anyway! Not only do the sustainable materials of green homes have a low environmental impact, but you'll also be saving a lot of money if you do. In the United States, for example, you could receive tax breaks by adding a little more green to your home, such as solar panels or a more efficient water heater. These don't even have to be massive changes to reduce your energy consumption. You could start by simply topping up the dirty clothes for the next laundry load.

You could potentially save hundreds on your bills by choosing to be sustainable. Purchasing energy-saving appliances, such as dishwashers, as well as water-saving plumbing systems (like that toilet I was talking about), would save you lots on your water.

An example of this would be a program run by the US Environmental Protection Agency (EPA). Their appliances save you money while ensuring that you're energy-efficient. So, next time you're out shopping, be sure to be on the lookout for the Energy Star label!

And if you happen to be one of those people flickering the switches, you can cut back on your electricity bill too. Switching to renewable sources, or deciding on green alternatives like LEDs, will save you considerable amounts of money and energy. And because you've got a more durable home, you'll be saving more money when it comes to the upkeep of your residence.

Plus, if you happen to run a business, going green could be just what you need. As I said, more people are jumping on board with eco-friendly firms, and if you market your business as one, more people will be lining up to buy your products.

With this increase of more and more eco-friendly businesses popping up, and consumers flooding through those doors, more money will stay in your community. See, when deciding to support and shop at local establishments, the community will grow and develop, ultimately, because of the economic boost.

Also, by choosing to eat local, organic, and seasonal products from your local supermarkets, you could boost the economy even more while also reducing greenhouse gas emissions in the process, because the food is local and doesn't need to be trucked in. And while you're at it, you'll become a healthier person due to their wholesome, unharmful traits.

With this smart-shopping system, and by cutting back to only purchasing the bare necessities, you'll be giving a helping hand in cleaning up the scrap and extending our resources, such as land, materials, and water. Our environment will be left cleaner and greener in no time!

And this is the fundamental purpose of what 'going green' means: cleaning up our planet and reducing pollution, energy consumption, carbon, and so forth. So, think green before you do anything. Carpool with a colleague or use public transport, and invest in eco-products, which will also reduce the amount of waste that falls to landfills.

A greener environment also means that everyone—you, your loved ones, and the critters—will live healthier in the days to come. The number of pollutants and toxins present in the air will be reduced, meaning that the air you're breathing will be left cleaner. And it's not just the park or beach you have to be thinking about. Indoors, the air quality of green homes is much cleaner, thanks to a lack of the volatility of chemicals like paint and cleansers.

The decrease of pollutants in the air not only means we will be breathing cleaner. Climate change will slow down, and water pollution will drop by reducing acid rain and eutrophication (excessive richness of nutrients in water bodies due to runoff, which can cause growth that chokes the plant and animal life in the water). Another way that water pollution can be fought is through waste reduction, like oils and pet waste, through green living, which also contributes to overcoming land pollution.

Moreover, these measures prevent health impacts, especially those in children, infants, and animals. And if you're a beauty lover or have skin problems, like acne, eco-friendly products could help. They're free from any toxic or harmful chemicals that, in the long run, will result in healthy skin.

Now that you've found the un-secret pill to excellent health, you'll note that you have more energy and that you're more productive at work and home. This is due to your body's immune system getting more robust at fighting off toxins present in our environment. And as you'll find later, recycling and producing new goods will, over time, help spark your creative side! You'll create new things from recycled goods and be on the lookout for new ways to live efficiently, so of course, this would reprogram your way of thinking, which is a good thing. And bonus, if you'd like to make a few bucks, you could always sell the recycled trinkets you make.

Green-living is a way of living that means you're more self-sufficient and independent because you're cutting yourself away from relying on fuels and other toxins. You're learning to create new and innovative ways to save energy and use renewable sources and other resources. You're breaking away from the unhealthy chain that drove us to this problem in the first place.

But, most importantly, you'll be creating a better environment to leave behind for those who follow, the future generation, your loved ones, and your children. You'll be standing as an example for others who will grow to appreciate the actions you took and how you genuinely cared for the environment.

These are all little steps we have to take that will impact the future greatly, allowing our planet to be around for a much longer time. Nature has been our guardian, looking after and taking care of us since the year dot, and now we have to return the favor. We owe the Earth that.

FOR THE LOVE OF GREEN

Now, what we've all been waiting for: ways you and I can jump in to support the environment by living greener lives. These are various ways you could consider taking on in your everyday life to ensure that you're applying greener practices to your routines. They're optional, and you don't have to employ all of them in your life right away. Pick and choose, and after a little while, you could add some more if you'd like. There are no rules in helping the environment, apart from not harming it, so try to make the most of it as best you can.

Taking Out the Trash

Many of us aren't in the position to make our community greener. We can't walk into grocery stores and demand that plastic bags be forbidden! Or that everyone brings along their own doggy-bag containers to restaurants. Going green, as I said, is a personal choice, meaning that you have to make sure that your part in the matter is clean. Apply greener practices in your life and around the home, while also carrying them around with you when you're out and about.

If you're like me, you love food. And that's why I thought it would be the appropriate place to start. Now, I've already mentioned the economic, environmental, and health boost that comes with shopping for local organic foods and when you shop as little as possible. I bring this up again because it truly is a great way to clean up the environment from trash and greenhouse gas. But, let's face it, not everyone wants to pop in the store and search around for local, organic foods. When you clock off at work, you simply want to grab and go.

Well, I have a proposition for you: why not skip the stones up the ladder by buying at least half of your things, or just some things, locally sourced from your local store. We know the benefits that come with it, but why is buying local valued? Because we want to cut back on our food miles, which is the distance food items have to cover to get from the producer to you. You have to consider the route all your goodies take to get to you, since more miles means more greenhouse gasses and fuel use. It takes a toll on our environment. So, if you do the opposite, you'll be reversing these food miles. Therefore, before you click checkout, think about how many food miles whatever you're buying would demand. Preferably, check in with your local farmers market for fresh, package-free foods, eat at a farm-to-table restaurant, and support local artists, clothing manufacturers, and retailers.

And while we're on the topic of shopping, another green-bagging tip is befriending your local butcher. Sounds weird, right? I know making a friend might seem more companionable than green. But, on the contrary, eating meat requires a lot of effort on our part if we want to do it sustainably. Besides, what's wrong with giving your butcher a hug?! By supporting them and asking questions, you could make your way up in a positive supply chain, possibly gaining access to the insides and extremities, such as kidneys, shanks, and glands of the animal, which offer much more flavor and possibilities than a fillet does anyway. But look, I know not everyone eats organs or feet. Whole-animal eating isn't to gross you out with guts and blood. It's about realizing that animals die for us to eat, and the least we could do is eat every part, not wasting anything, or else their death would have been for nothing.

But, honestly, the best option still remains to go vegan. This is a dreaded idea for many people I've noticed. A friend of mine even said he would rather starve than go vegan. It made no sense, of course, but still, his loathing of veganism and love for meat, fish, and dairy was made very clear! Going vegan is a way to reduce greenhouse gas emissions and energy consumption, it's a fact. You could flatten your carbon footprint by 73% when you incorporate this cleaner diet, stated an independent article (Paskill, 2020).

And a quick hack I've learned is to compost on the go, not just when you're at home. Take your own lunch to work with your own container, so you could have a mini-compost carrier while also reducing the packaging waste from lunch deliveries. Throughout the day, you could stack up on your apple cores, fruit peels, tea bags, crusts, and even cardboard or tissue scraps. When you get home, you can simply add it to the pile.

But let's move on from the food before we all end up hungry! A big part of cleaning up the environment is choosing to clean green, and no, I'm not talking about the product. In the simplest terms, green-cleaning means using cleaning methods and products that are safer for us and the environment. You'll be right on track by ditching harmful chemicals! Instead, go for chemical-free lawn and garden care, natural beauty and hygiene items, and natural household cleaners.

Typical green-cleaning products characteristics are:

- No phosphates or chlorine

- No artificial fragrances and colors
- Organically grown ingredients using sustainable farming practices
- Biodegradable or recyclable packaging

But you see, green-cleaning, in my opinion, is also widely how you manage your trash. We all know recycling is *the* green practice we all know. But I'll focus on that later on. It's more than simply throwing away wisely and keeping printing to the bare unavoidable, both of which are relevant.

It's about dumping things we would ordinarily do, like our use of paper. If you stick to doing more things online, like sending emails, saving files on your computer, and so forth, you'll reduce your own paper use. We live in a modern world where technological advancements are at the forefront, after all. Why not join in? This will dramatically reduce paper waste and the need to cut down more trees. But, remember to turn off the computers, other appliances, and lights when you clock out as well.

And while we're at it, remember to keep an eye out for your electrical appliances and electronics, like your laptop, mobile, and white goods like fridges. Clean them regularly, and you'll prolong its life. This will lessen the chances of them being thrown out, which has a huge carbon impact. If it's really time to wish the item well and it's beyond repairs, call the manufacturer or company of purchase to see whether they take back items for reuse or recycling. If not, dispose of your lost-cause goods properly.

And here I go again, sounding like a parrot who only knows one word. Eco-driving everyone! But come on, it's such an environmentally saving concept of going green. Cars are harming the environment, and we're a species that's constantly up and moving from place to place. I mean, if the air could speak, it would only cough.

So, whenever you need to be somewhere, think to yourself: What other options do I have? Can you catch a lift with someone else, take a train or bus, walk, jog, or cycle? Go for the greener options, always. And if it's not necessary to go anywhere, then stay inside for the day! With the tech revolution I mentioned, it's always possible to Skype or call instead.

The Bathroom Hamper

Everything above applies to most of the rooms in your home. Everything green works together, like some single-colored Rubik's cube that is endless. But I would like to divert our attention to the bathroom and wardrobe for now.

Let's start with your closet. Buying used clothing is a sustainable steal for ramping up your drawers. But I won't give away too much since I've already dedicated an entire chapter all about thrifting! What I would like to do now is bring up a way of shopping people rarely know about: *swishing*. I know it might sound like this belongs more in the bathroom than it does in the bedroom, but bear with me!

Swishing is when you bag up all your unwanted clothes and tag them along to a store or event for swishing. You then swap your clothes for credit, which could be used to buy items that others traded-in. It's a greener way to revive and polish your wardrobe by bartering pieces. Remember when you were younger, and you would swap playing cards or other collectible toys amongst your peers? It's like that, only it's a way of living and dressing.

And a quick word of advice: choose your materials carefully. Some fabrics age and hold better than others. Buying leather and denim, for example, is a much better option when pre-owned because of the material's durability and longevity, and they often look better once worn anyway!

Also, it wouldn't hurt to learn a few mending tricks here and there. Take a few lessons and invest in a sewing machine so that you can learn how to tailor your baggy clothes to fit like a glove. And learn how to sew on a button with the old needle and thread. This will save many of your favorites from losing their place on the hangers! You can also make socks from yarn and aprons from pieces of denim. Be creative and reuse as much as you can.

Okay, but let's 'zip' this up. When I say recycle, you automatically think about kitchen waste: your fruits, soda cans, and wrappers. And this is correct since 90% of us recycle our kitchen waste. But what about our beauty product's packaging? If you do, then you're only one out of the 50% that does. So, add a post-it to the mirror to remind you to add it to the bins too. And why not drop the disposables while you're at it? Cotton wool, for example, takes an enormous amount of water to, well, be cotton. It's not worth it. For the cosmetic lovers out there, opt for reusable discs to remove make-up. And purchase facial cleansers or exfoliating gloves for that extra cleanse!

And, I'll only say this once: I beg you, don't fall for the siren call of the minis! These travel-sized beauty products might seem cute, but they're honestly a huge amount of waste for no reason, and the amount of product you get isn't worth it. I always fell for those little guys, but now, I've converted to buying full-sized, refillable bottles instead, and they last for months.

So, when it comes to your lavatory, pick up after yourself and recycle, choose sustainable, eco-friendly products and tools, and don't play with the water in there! In the bedroom, go second-hand, and learn some new clothes-saving skills. It's simple to do a few things here and there that will make a huge difference.

Green Thumb

If I seem really excited, I do apologize. I've recently taken it upon myself to widen the area I use for gardening, you see, and it really has been a fantastic thrill! I've been waiting throughout to talk about some greener gardening approaches with you.

The first thing I was told was to clean the air. You can never have enough plants in your home, and some of them are extremely helpful to have around (well, all plants are).

- Mother-in-law's tongue gives oxygen off at night. It's a perfect fit for the bedroom.
- Peace lilies and Boston ferns can reduce mold spores in the air, so assign them to the bathroom.
- Weeping figs are best at removing formaldehyde, a strong-smelling, colorless gas, from carpets and furniture so they can flourish in the living room.

Now, as we step outside, the first thing I would like to do is refer back to being local. This time, being local encourages you to buy and grow your own local flowers. About 90% of United Kingdom flowers sold through florists are imported (Berrill et al., 2020). The same counts for air as it does for food: we've got to slim down on our air miles as much as we can. Find a local floral supplier or independent flower growers who can supply you with native plants that are right for your location's current conditions. If you live in a generally dry area or there's a drought, focus on xerophytes (drier, desert plants) like cacti instead of Dahlias, which require a lot of water. Maybe cultivate a desert garden rather than insisting on a green lawn you have to water (you'd be surprised at how beautiful desert plant blooms can be!). And if the plants need to be imported, first look at which local, native plants are around. Alternatively, you could also grow your own flowers to pluck when needed or just to lock up carbon.

Ah yes, this shoots us right into our following discussion: bolting up more carbon. No, not all of us have room for large trees. The basic principle isn't about having tall trees around but an abundance of vegetation. So the fuller your garden, the better! You could also try stacking log piles as dividers between the garden bed and grass since they also lock up carbon while they decay, which could take years. And if you do have a lawn, let your grass grow long between cuts! It not only saves gas and electricity, therefore reducing carbon emissions, it also allows wildlife to explore through the tiny forests of the suburbs.

And be sure to cheer on these critters, like hedgehogs who eat caterpillars, slugs, and snails which you could provide, considering there would be more creeping around in your garden. Also, by planting clumps of flowers, pollinators, like bees, would visit and it would make it easier for them to fly between trips. For example, Bee balm is, ironically, a favorite amongst the winged workers.

Living greener and greener ways to live is really about thinking of what you're doing and then asking yourself, "Am I helping or harming the environment?"

Look, we're consumers, and there's power in that. The power lies, simply put, in our *choices*. We have the pick to decide where we'll spend our hard-earned dough. Spend it wisely, though, and choose the proper goods, services, and experiences that will leave behind a smaller carbon footprint. The world will send you a thank you card later!

Money talks; some would argue that it's the language of the world. Without it, we can't go on, because our species is driven with currency and trade, always has been. So, if we were to put our heads together and use this purchasing power for the greater good, we would create a demand for more sustainable practices. Those who don't apply themselves will be left behind.

A CRASH COURSE ON RECYCLING

What Is Recycling?

We've all heard about it, or the word at least rings a bell. Waste materials, such as papers and plastics, are set aside, later on, to be twisted into newer materials and objects, or sometimes into energy.

Let's say your garbage is a load of laundry in the washing machine. Recycling would be the inner-drum, the thing you can see that spins around inside the machine. Thus, it's a cycle or process of reusing what we've already used where, for example, soda cans are turned into soda cans. Some things like straws, however, can't be recycled again.

The Three Types of Recycling

As suggested above, there are three types of recycling. They're like big boxes, where their content would be all the recyclables, like glass, which falls into these three types.

- *Primary Recycling*: This is where the recyclable materials could be reused without changing their current state. It mostly ends up being used for what it was created for, a jar for a jar. These recyclables shouldn't be modified in any way, like broken down. You could also use, sell, or donate them. For example, glass jars might be used as drinking glasses. Toys could be donated to charity or handed down to other friends and families with kids. Electronics could be donated or used for parts.
- *Secondary Recycling*: With this type of recycling, the recycled material may be reused differently than it started out. This is often the case with do-it-yourself (DIY) crafts. For example, egg cartons could be used for seedlings, or plastic bottles could be used for planting.
- *Tertiary Recycling*: This recycling involves the altering of materials through chemicals to make them reusable, which could be both internal or external. Internal recycling is where recyclable materials are recovered from the public. External collections are recovered within factories and other manufacturing facilities.

What Can You Recycle?

Recyclable Material

Recyclable Material	Example
Paper	Newspapers, magazines, and other mixed papers.
Cardboard	Corrugated cardboard and grey paperboard, like those used for packaging and paper boxes or like egg cartons.
Plastic	Soda and water bottles, milk containers, product containers, PVC pipes, sandwich bags, yogurt tubs, Styrofoam.
Clothing	Clothing made with cotton, wool, and silk without synthetic fibers, such as polyester and buttons, labels, and zippers.
Textiles	Industrial rags, low-grade blankets, insulation materials, and upholsteries.
E-Waste	Computers, mobile phones, tables, TVs, stereos, copy-machine, printers, fax machines, gaming consoles.
Wood	Pallets, boxes, floorboards, chipboards, fencing, plywood, furniture.
Glass	Bottle, jars, windows, drinkware, computer screens.
Bricks and inert waste	Bricks, cement, sand.
Metals	Tin, aluminum, and steel.

What Makes Something Recyclable?

Now, you should know that the above account was only a brief overview of materials you could recycle, an elementary list if you must. There are much smaller, sometimes intricate, details in recycling. Some materials, for instance, are stubborn to recycle, like styrofoam, which isn't as easy and usually not accepted at most recycling facilities. And there are also other recyclable options, like food waste, which can be composted, and water.

But what exactly makes something recyclable in the first place? Rubicon stated that for an item to be recycled within a city, three key areas had to align, specifically:

- Technology must exist to recycle the material.
- There must be a buyer.
- The economics must work for the processor.

To sum up these areas, I would say that for an item to be recycled, the technology to break down the product into raw material to be used again must be available. Anything could be recycled as long as there's an interested buyer at the end of it all. And then, we have materials recovery facilities. They have a certain threshold in terms of critical mass that they need to economically recover a material. Which, simply put, means that if they don't get enough pieces of a material, like some sort of plastic, it would be economically better for them to dispose of the batches as landfill waste. Recycling is seen as a business. I mean, look at what was said: you need the proper equipment, interested customers, demand for goods, and enough stock to make the costs and labor worth it. It's business.

Trash Recycling Steps

1. Consumers provide the materials.
2. Haulers collect the materials.
3. Materials are sorted.
4. Reprocessors accept repurposing materials.
5. Materials are finalized and sent off to markets.

So, there you have it! Now, let's move on to other ways to handle what we no longer need.

REDUCE, REUSE, RECYCLE

I rode my bike up a hill today. You can say I was really ...

UP-CYCLING

If you're like me, your house is probably stacked with all sorts of goodies that Sherlock Holmes couldn't even make sense of! But, we're too busy, lazy, sentimental, or forgetful to clean up the crime scene. I get it! I really do. But, sometimes, a little inspiration and a read or two is just what you need to repurpose, reuse, and up-cycle your old things. Look at that case of old CDs. Does it still have a glimpse of life? Yes! There are so many crafts and other uses for almost everything. So, grab the paint, close the lid on the bins, and let your creative side in!

REUSING THE USUAL RUBBISH

Our goal should be to let nothing go to waste! But, some things are beyond saving, I agree. Still, these scraps should, preferably, be pulled into biodegradable trash bags, which degrades much faster than your traditional, impossible-to-open, plastic ones. Ah, this swoops me off to our first item of interest.

That's right, we're back on the plastic! And still, my opinion is the same: landfills should have a restraining order against plastics. But the good news is, we could help keep these plastic perpetrators at bay by simply not buying them or, if that's unavoidable, reusing them!

The most apparent reuse technique by far is using them for their intended purpose. Stuff the bags into your trunk or cubby so you'll always have them when you're out shopping. Grabbing them before entering the store, however, is where the obstacle steps in. You're re-reading your grocery list in your head, entirely forgetting Mr.Plastic in the backseat. Don't worry about it. If it's necessary to get a bag, just pop it in with the rest of them. When your stash starts to take up too much trunk space, you can simply sort them before making your next move. The bags that aren't ripped or torn could be donated to local businesses, like thrift shops, animal shelters, and libraries. And, although I recommend finding other uses first before recycling them right away, you could still go for it. Many stores have designated boxes for recycling close by their doors. But the best option for using bags for shopping is to ditch them altogether. As I said before, reusable bags are just considerably better.

But let's say you haven't gone cloth yet, or you still have a couple of plastic bags lying around. What else is there to do with them?

Well, suppose you're moving or you plan on storing away a few breakables. Instead of going out to buy packing materials, work with what you've got. Pack valuables inside plastic bags or put a layer of them between your things. It will protect your items and add extra padding for those rough roads or restless rats. And you guessed it! The same goes for any fragile packages you have to mail out for someone.

Another great use for plastic bags is to clamp down on heat, steam, and moisture. What do I mean? First, if you plan on going out of town, placing bags around your plants can trap moisture, thus keeping them alive while you're away. They can act as a mini-greenhouse. As for heat, it's more for wiper and mirror protection against the freezing weather. And finally, one I use all the time: trapping steam for pre-cooking potatoes. I know it sounds mad, but simply clean out a bag (wash it out well), peel, cut, water, and season potatoes, before dropping them into the bag with a loose knot at the top. Leave in the microwave for about 5 minutes or more. It works like a charm, and making mash for dinner has never been faster!

Now, let's not stray too far away from 'bags' just yet, although, this one you don't carry around on your shoulder —I hope. Believe it or not, you could do so much with them: I'm talking about tea bags! Yes, these little baggies aren't just useful for a drink. But, after you've brewed yourself a cup, chill the bags in the fridge, then place one over each eye to relieve puffiness or onto insect bites and minor burns to soothe the skin. And if you need a full-body treatment, you can add the bags to your bath to smooth out the skin while overdosing on therapeutic scents. Tea also works wonders for plants: simply break open the bag and sprinkle the content over the soil below the plants to feed and rejuvenate them. See? Nothing is too small to reuse or recycle!

Coffee grounds also have the same garden-nurturing benefits. They could be used to keep pests, such as ants, away and are great for seedlings and plants like roses because of their richness in nitrogen. And if you happen to have a few beans left, ground them up and stick them in the freezer to neutralize any odors.

And these caffeinated drinks aren't the only scraps we can make use of. Eggshells are also great growth boosters for plants, but that's not all they're helpful for. You could grind them up and add them to your smoothies and shakes, along with some grounded avocado seeds. I know it sounds a bit cringy, but it's not. Some might say it's a taste to get used to, some wouldn't notice, and others will enjoy it. The point is, it will surely spike your calcium and fiber while loading you up with antioxidants.

Other healthy pieces we usually toss are orange and lemon peels. Little did I know that when dried out for at least a week and then combined with water and vinegar, this tonic is a phenomenal homemade multi-purpose cleaner.

And then we get down to the oily mess known as bacon grease. And although we do usually drain it down, it could still be used for cooking. Simply keep it in the fridge, screwed shut, to prevent oxidation, and then you're ready for whenever a recipe screams for butter or oil or a little extra of that yummy bacon flavor.

Another use that I found rather interesting was making candles from the grease! You can pop it in the fridge till it hardens, which usually takes up to 2 hours, before drilling a hole in the center and adding a natural wick. Then it's ready to light up! But, if you're in the process of becoming vegan, and other members of the family aren't, I wouldn't recommend lighting it because that bacon smell will be all over.

For both of the above, I would recommend using glass jars, because not only are these excellent containers, you'll be taking double shifts at living greener! And these jars could really be used for almost anything: multiple DIY projects and crafts, getting organized around the home like storing spices, pasta, elastics, spare change, nuts, and bolts, you name it! Or, you could simply fill jars up with water for refreshing sips on those warm days or after a jog.

Another glass-related item is the wine bottle, well, not the bottle itself but the corks. Let's crawl back to the garden, where old corks can be used as waterproof markers for your plants. Write the plant's name on it and jab a kebab stick or chopstick in there before sticking it in by the plant. And if the corks aren't rubber or plastic, you can also blend the cork before spreading it across your landscape. This will help retain water and keep your plants moist.

But, for the DIY-buffs out there, you can carve a design into the top and dip it into an ink pad—and there you have yourself a stamp! Or a needle holder if you prefer sewing for fun. But, if you don't have the time, corks could also be pitched into those designated boxes for donations and recycling.

And you know that these are only a few examples of alternatively using things we would usually chuck. You could use paper towel rolls to organize cables and holiday lights to keep them from tangling, or turn them into lint rollers. Styrofoam, the plastic that's so hard to recycle, could easily be reused as stencils for paintings, drainage for plants, or packing peanuts.

Everything still has a bit of life brimming inside of it. You just have to peek closer and uncover a way to give it a new purpose!

THE ABCS OF COMPOSTING

Composting is a great way to reduce waste and greenhouse gas emissions. "But it stinks, doesn't it?" "I don't want that stench around my home, and it's hard to do anyway!" Actually… no! Get away from *that* misleading mindset. Composting is really not that hard to do. And yes, compost is decaying organic matter, but the smell isn't that bad. I have a bin in the backyard myself. You'll have a nutrient-rich garden bursting with growth in no time, while giving the environment a cheering shout from the bleachers.

Building Blocks of Composting at Home

First up, we've got our fundamental ingredients: our browns, greens, and water. It's pretty simple to differentiate and remember the difference between your browns and your greens. Brown are dead leaves, branches, and twigs, everything brown. Your greens are grass clippings, vegetables, and fruit scraps, and coffee grounds (yeah, I know, it's brown but in this case it's really green). Not everything is green, but it's still easy to learn, or you could simply make notes for yourself. Your pile should have an equal amount of brown to greens because brown provides your heap with carbon, and greens provide nitrogen. Water is the ingredient that moistens the whole deal so that everything can be broken down. Look at the chart below to make it easier. I have included some detailed examples for you to see if it applies to your situation.

Clear for Compost

Loads of Green	Buckets of Brown
Fruit and vegetable peels	Shredded newspaper
Coffee grounds	Bedding from chickens
Eggshells	Wood chips
Fresh leaves	Shredded, non-glossy junk mail
Grass clippings	Bedding from hamsters, guinea pigs, rabbits
Melon rinds	Used napkins
Houseplant trimmings	Pinecones
Seaweed	Chopped up twigs and small branches
Weeds that haven't gone to seed	Fall leaves
Tea leaves and paper tea bags	Shredded office or school papers
Old vegetables that aren't suitable for eating anymore	Brown paper shopping bags, shredded or torn
Deadheads from flowers	Straw
Dead plants (as long as they aren't diseased)	Toilet paper, paper towel, or wrapping paper tubes
Cooked plain rice	Coir liners for hanging baskets
Stale bread	Sawdust (only from untreated wood)
Broccoli stalks	Fallen bird's nests
Cooked plain pasta	Used paper coffee filters
Corn cobs	Pine needles
Corn husks	Excelsior
Sod that you've removed to make new garden beds	Pressed paper egg cartons, torn into small pieces
Citrus rinds	Raffia
Thinnings from the vegetable garden	Leftover peat or coir from seed starting
Old dried herbs and spices that have lost their flavor	Brown paper lunch bags, shredded or torn
Spent bulbs that you used for forcing indoors	Nutshells (avoid walnut shells as they can inhibit plant growth)
Holiday greenery from wreaths and swags (just be sure to cut the stems off of the wreath or wires first)	Torn up plain corrugated cardboard boxes (not with glossy coatings)

No-Go for Compost

Release harmful substances that could:

Harm plants:

- Black walnut tree leaves or twigs
- Coal or charcoal ash

Will make compost reek and attracts pests, such as rodents and flies:

- Dairy products and eggs
- Fats, grease, lard, or oils
- Meat or fish bones and scraps

Or cause harm in other ways, so leave out:

- Plants ridden with insects or diseases that could transfer to other plants.
- Pet waste, like cat and dog feces and cat litter, which could contain bacteria, germs, parasites, and viruses that are harmful to humans.
- Yard trimmings treated with chemical pesticides, which could kill beneficial composting organisms.

Setting up Camp

Setting up shop for your compost is actually easy. It starts with choosing where you want and can set up roots for your compost bin or pile. If you live in an apartment building, for example, I doubt that you'll be able to claim the front lawn as your own waste mountain. Lucky for us, composting isn't limited to the outdoors!

You can still compost materials indoors when using a particular type of bin that you can pick up at your local gardening supply store or hardware store. You could even try making one yourself!

But remember to keep an eye out for what you're throwing in and tend to your stack. When you properly manage your compost bin, pests and rodents won't be tempted by it, and there won't be a lingering foul smell, both being things we want to avoid, especially when inside.

Below are instructions of how to build your own compost bin. It should be simple for you to make and will definitely be cost effective and fun!

DIY to the Rescue: Build your own domesticated compost bin!

Gather up the following:

- Container with lid (plastic is excellent for reusing, but you could also use stainless steel or bamboo bins if you'd like)
- Nylon mesh screen
- Drill
- Hot glue gun
- Dirt
- Kitchen scraps
- Shredded newspapers

Bin builder:

1. Drill five evenly spaced holes into the lid.
2. This will help with ventilation and airflow, which is necessary for materials to break down.
3. Add the nylon mesh screen.
4. Measure how large the lid is, and cut a large enough chunk of the nylon to cover the air holes. Hot glue the screen to the underside of the container lid. This will keep insects from getting in and out of the bin.
5. Start filling in the bin.

6. Start with a layer of dirt on the bottom and the shredded newspapers on top of that. Then drop in the kitchen scraps. Try breaking these scraps up into smaller pieces so that it decomposes quicker.
7. Stir the pot.
8. Add some water before stirring the mixture, and repeat this about once a week. Be sure to put the lid back on, or else you might walk into a bug infestation!

However, when you're able to compost outside, great! Still, that comes with its own set of rules. First up is choosing the right spot to set up your compost roots, steering towards a dry, shady spot near a water source. And, although optional, cover the top of your compost with a tarp. This will help keep your pile damp and hopefully deter critters. Stop off at your heap to add in collected brown and green materials as you go along, watering them after you've added them. Do this every week or two.

Composting can take anywhere from 2 months to 2 years, so don't expect it to happen overnight or think that you're doing it wrong if it starts at a standstill. Just be patient and wait it out.

Useful composting toolbox:

- Pitchforks
- Square-point shovel
- Machete
- Water hoses with spray head
- Scissors or blender for breaking up waste

Pile Problems

Sometimes, the best composters still stumble upon problems, and the best you can do is try and step on the breaks. If you're struggling with the one problem feared from the start, don't worry: the smell can be controlled more easily than you think. If the stench comes around, throw in some more dried leaves and shredded newspaper to the pile. This will help balance out the ratio of content and could control the odors.

And in second place on our feared list: infestation of pests and rodents. It all starts with your choice of containers. For some an open compost is fine, especially if it's away from the house. But if animals and insects are a potential issue, a solid bin with a lid that keeps insects out is the only way to go. Also, avoid adding meats, dairy, and fats, as said before.

And if you're growing impatient with the time it takes for your compost to decompose, I regret to inform you that there's no easy way around it. You should simply keep repeating the same routine, stirring and watering the pile once a week, and keep the contents cut up and small to speed things up a bit.

THE ART OF SCRAPS

We've been talking about reusing your old waste for the greater good throughout. But, as my father used to say, "I don't have a creative bone in my body. If someone were ever to find my bones, all they would see is grey!" Dramatic, I know. But he had a great point. Some people simply have no idea where to start crafting, painting, or building little trinkets, let alone crafts from their rubbish.

But that's why I'm here! To slap you with some inspiration and ideas to help kick-start your creative side!

For me, it all started with my parents. When the holidays were knocking at our door, they would scatter around the house for empty boxes of cookies, nuggets, eggs, and cereal. These cardboard food containers would soon be wrapped up to hold our gifts. I remember how we would always sit around the tree, joking about how we had scored chicken nuggets for Christmas! The tradition, joke included, has been passed down to our children since. But it didn't end there for me. You see, when I grew up, recycling and reusing followed me. I mean, I married into it!

In the holidays, when I'm glad to indulge in all the chocolates and biscuits, my wife, on the other hand, gets excited about the containers! A new jewelry box! she might exclaim. Ferrero Rocher is by far her favorite among them all. It already has a few slots where the chocolate used to be, and it's delicately decorated with gold with a clear lid sealing the deal. It even sounds exotic and foreign (*What are you wearing? Ferrero Rocher*). She stores her earrings, necklaces, bracelets, and rings, with a proud smile plastered on her face.

But, she also uses others, don't get me wrong. Like those tin boxes that biscuits come in. There are multiple in our home right now, standing tall as memory boxes, knitting supply carriers, and a small storage box for anything from batteries to receipts.

We all have also helped other members of my family dapple with used goods and art. Take my nephew's school project, for example. The school had organized a market where the kids had to set up shop. It was to teach them about creating business plans and seeing how profitable companies work.

His grand idea was a DIY ornament business since it was close to Christmas time. We all jumped in to help! And I was hungry for a challenge. Deciding to wing it, I grabbed some scrap papers and cardboard before getting right to it. My end project was the Golden Snitch from the Harry Potter Series. J. K. Rowling would've been proud! And not to toot my own horn, but it ended up being sold for $15!

These are just small everyday things we end up tossing when we see no use for them, while in the meantime, there's still so much life and potential beauty in them. We just have to look further than the conventional opinion that trash is nothing but trash.

Guided DIYs

Light Bulb Lamp

I stumbled upon this great idea on the Instructables Workshop site (www.instructables.com). Do you have any old light bulbs lying around the home? Well, now is as good a time as any to gather them up for an aesthetic candle that will light up your home like no other!

Supplies:

- Your bulb(s), but make sure they're clean
- A cotton shoelace
- A metal bottle cap
- A washer/spacer that's quite large
- Small magnets, two of them

From your toolbox:

- Drill/punch
- Drill bit that's a little smaller than the shoelace
- Lamp oil
- Tape
- Water

- Granular Substance (Preferably sand because it's more abrasive)

The disassemble:

1. Tap the bottom of the bulb (not too hard) until the black glass is broken.
2. Then, tap the inner stem of the bulb with the wire in it. Extract the insides.
3. Grab the sand and pour some into the bulb, add water and swoosh the mixture. around. As you're swirling, you'll notice the inner white coating shedding off.
4. Rinse the bulb intensively after the white coating has completely peeled off.
5. Set it to the side, we'll get back to it later on.

The cap:

1. Grab the cap and shoelace.
2. Drill a hole in the center of the cap. The hole should be just under the breadth of the lace, so start small to avoid ending up with a crater!
3. Tape the middle of the shoelace (at the tapping band) to avoid unraveled, worn edges when you cut it. (Then you can cut the lace.)
4. Thread the taped end into the bottle cap and pull it through.
5. Screw the duo onto the lightbulb's cap.
6. You want enough slack at the bottom, so do a measuring test.
7. Take off the cap, and find your magnets (I'm sure they'll be together!)

The base:

1. With your washer/spacer ready, stick some tape onto the one side.
2. Flick the washer over and center a magnet on the tape.
3. Cut more tape and stick it on the other side, sealing the magnet.

The finishing touches:

1. Throw your other magnet into the bulb (gently) and set the bulb onto the base.
2. Carefully pour 2/3 tsp of lamp oil into the bulb.
3. Find your cap, complete with your shoelace wick, and seal the whole deal.
4. There shouldn't be more than ½ of an inch of lace peeking out at the top.
5. Light it up!

And that's it! Save your breath for when you have to extinguish the flame (It tends to require quite the lungful!).

But if you're more into snow globes, then you can ditch the lamp oil and wick. Instead, gather some toys, crushed eggshells, glycerin, clear aqua silicone, or waterproof glue. Combine all of these into the bulb, seal it up with a bottle cap, and you're set to go!

Suitcase Side Tables

Ever since I saw this craft by Kim Moreau from Good Housekeeping I've been unpacking all my suitcases just for a little more coffee (and foot) space! And if you've been looking to add a bit of retro flair to your home, grab your grandfather's old suitcase or pick one up at the thrift store and follow my lead!

Bag up:

- Old hard-shell suitcase
- Four table legs painted to match your case
- Four angled top plates and 16 screws
- Particleboard or medium density fiberboard (MDF) (cut to fit suitcase)
- Jigsaw (only if you want to cut the particleboard/MDF yourself)
- Drill

All about the base:

1. While you're at the thrift store, swing by the hardware store to pick up a piece of particleboard or MDF (and of course everything you don't have lying around).
2. You can ask if they would cut it to the right size for you or you could do it by yourself with a jigsaw. Just remember to pay attention to the suitcase's frame, angling the corners down to fit the edges thereof.

Adding top plates:

1. Place the cut-out on top of a tall stool or table and the suitcase on top of that. The suitcase bottom will push down on the board, fastening it so that you can drill the plates.
2. Place a top plate in each corner of the suitcase, before securing them with screws. These screws should be long enough to go through all the layers (plates,

suitcase, and board). Make sure that all of them are in place.

Speed walking: Stick the legs onto the plates through the center holes and twist them on, and you're done!

Also, remember that your creativity isn't limited to these steps alone. You could, for example, pick up some leather paint while you're still at the shop and go to town with colors, designs, glitters, and fabrics that you want to try out! But there you have it, your new antique-like, chic addition to your furniture. So start stacking cups, mugs, and your favorite books on top!

Mirror, Mirror on the Wall

Mary Smith from onehowto.com has really shown me that, with a bit of imagination, you could even turn a tennis racket into a beautiful mirror to compliment your walls.

In the sports bag:

- Tennis racket
- Mirror (make sure to measure the size of the mirror beforehand)
- Sandpaper (with a fine grain.)
- Paint
- Varnish
- Closed eye bolt

The game:

1. Without hurting or bending the frame, snap off the strings carefully.
2. Sand down the racket and polish it up.

3. Once polished to perfection, you can paint or decorate it as you wish.
4. When everything is dry, varnish your racket for a better overall look.
5. Glue an oval-shaped mirror in your racket.
6. You could also place a wooden plank or other resistant material at the back with mirror adhesive to let it stay in place.
7. When the glue sets, you only have one step left. Add a closed eye bolt on top of the racket to hang it on the wall.

And now you'll be looking fine! And when it comes to mirrors, you can really use so many other things to glam up your home, from old bicycles to old doors. Basically, everything if you put your mind to it.

Coat Hooks From Spoons

In the bowl:

- Spoons (as many as you want; You could also use any utensils, such as a fork, really. Just make sure they've got sturdy handles)
- A slightly rounded hammer and something to use as an anvil
- Screws and something to drive them in
- A drill
- Material to attach hooks to, like wall, or a slab of wood (you can paint it nicer beforehand)

Flatten the spoons: With the hammer, flatten your spoons, trying not to put too many nasty-looking dents in them.

Bending: Try bending a nice hook shape, in the end it should look like a slide, or steep slope.

Drilling: Drill holes into the top of your spoons. This, for me, is perfectly fine, but you're more than welcome to add more holes, or change their positioning.

Finished: Simply screw your hooks onto their final pieces, then it's done! Ready to wear some hats and jackets!

And these wall hooks don't just have to be made from cutlery, as you might have realized most crafts can be reused on other objects. You could also use wrenches in the same concept and bend them to your liking. I also saw a valve coat rack, which looked pretty amazing! So, if you happen to have that lying around, you're in luck, because I don't, and I'll be rather jealous in the end.

Cereal Notebook

Thanks to Creme de la Craft (www.cremedelacraft.com), you could stop buying all those notebooks, and, instead, make your own! I know we're trying to stop using paper and boxes for things that we might have to throw away someday, but sometimes your kids need a notebook or two for school, or perhaps you would like to start a journal for them, which you could keep inside of a memory box, or maybe you're still just a fan of keeping a journal! But with the latter, I would say that you either still hold onto these notebooks or use both the paper and box for a compost pile or some other craft you have up your sleeve. Just as another green 101!

Dot it down:

- Cereal box (1 cereal box equals 2 notebooks); alternatively, you can use cardboard, cardstock, or gift boxes as well

- Paper for the insides (I used 8.5" x 11" lined paper, but you can use any kind and size you'd like)
- Decorative paper (small piece to cover the spine.)
- Button
- Pen
- Ruler
- Scissors
- Needle
- Embroidery floss

The steps:

1. Cut out the cereal box to create the cover for your notebook. Mine, for example, would be 5.5" x 8", but you can go with any size you would like.
2. Fold the cut-out piece in half so that the blank (brown) side is facing out.
3. Thread the embroidery floss through the needle and sew on the button to the front of the notebook. Leave thread hanging, about 20 inches. This will be used as a band that wraps around the book and button to close the notebook.
4. To cover the images of the product inside, glue or tape paper to the inside. If it's sticking out at the edges, simply cut it to fit.
5. Then grab the rest of your papers and give them a trim, so that they're smaller than your cover.
6. With the embroidery floss and needle in hand, stitch the paper to the notebook, running down the spine.
7. When done, glue or tape your decorative paper to the spine.
8. You can gently cut the edges of the notebook to form round corners, but that's optional.

9. Then you're set to decorate the notebook to your desire!

And I know I didn't mention the ruler, but that's just for the measurements, and for you afterwards. There you have it, now you just need some pens, and you're on your way!

The Crafts Are in Your Hands

I wish I had all day to give you billions of crafts step-by-step. But seriously, look around the space you're sitting at right now. Go on, look!

Do you see a tin can, glass jar, plastic bottle, metal caps, or cardboard box? Well, there you have some excellent supplies already! Remember this: your world is your craft store, so shop around until you drop! Hunt down some new ideas and inspiration on the web, or ask around for some ideas.

Metal caps could become fridge magnets, and don't get me started on the endless possibilities of tin cans and jars: from planters, cutlery holders, centerpieces, lunch boxes, you name it, and most likely, it's a yes! And besides, you need no validation or approval for a craft. It's your design, idea, and project. Don't let anyone tell you that it's a bad or strange idea (unless it's harmful, of course).

Crafting these DIY projects isn't about who can do it the best. It's not about how beautiful others find it or how long it takes for you to manage to paint a tin can without it flaking off in seconds. It's about giving new life to things that would, usually, end up next to the food scraps in a junkyard. While also, yes, glamming up your living space, yourself, and your social media accounts! It's also a wonderful way to teach the children in your life how to reuse things and be creative, not to mention the quality time you get to spend with them. It's a simple game of win–win!

If I could give you one prominent piece of advice when it comes to making your DIYs more meaningful and fun, it's this: always remember that life's too short to do it alone. I don't mean to be a dark and gloomy downer all of a sudden, but this is a life-hack we've all probably heard along the road; you only learn to appreciate this with the years and grey hairs.

One of my fondest memories of making trash into something strange yet remarkable was with my grandfather. We used to go from restaurant to restaurant and store to store asking for soda cans and spare parts like wheel nuts. When we got back home, we would hit the garage. Two men (although I was just a little boy) hard at work! We would cut the soda cans into wings and propellers, sticking on spare parts here and there. Soon, I was outside with my cousins and sister, flying around airplanes! It will always be a memory that sticks with me. And I've made it my occupation to ensure that my kids have the chance to share in such memories.

But before that, I grew older, always trying to be independent. I mean, you pretty much think you've got the whole world figured out. But I missed home. And whenever I was there, I always cherished making small trinkets and things from rubbish. My parents were real Van Gogh's when it came to creating something from absolutely nothing. I didn't quite get the talent, but I still try, and my wife is of great help. She's the talent and I'm the cheerleader in those scenarios!

The point is that when you include those closest to you, creating crafts becomes effortless. If it looks beautiful, you'll share an *aww*, and if it turns out looking horrible, you'll share a laugh. It's genuinely just a great way to get in some bonding time with your folks, grandparents, spouse, children, family, and friends. No one ever said that being eco-friendly had to be hard work all the time, right?

And at times when you're crafting alone, still uninspired and lost, even after looking at what feels like thousands of online pictures and step-by-step articles. Go take a rest and sit down. Take with you a jug, jar, box, or can, and just go crazy with it! Without an idea or plan sketched out, just do whatever comes to mind. Paint the sides, flip it over, cut something there, stick some gems here, or paper mâché the whole thing if you want. Whatever you end up doing, it will help give you a running start for your imagination. And don't mind how it turns out. Keep it around to remind you of what a Picasso you really are! You'll definitely get out some frustrations, relax, and make a change one paint stroke at a time. And when you're done you could always store your things in a craft supply jar! (Which is exactly as the name sounds like: a glass jar, decorated to your liking, stuffed with glitter, glues, and all that.

5

BEING THRIFTY

What happens if you sell a used watch? It becomes ...

SECOND HANDED

My sister and I were sitting in the car on our way to pick up some things. She needed some new clothes and shoes for the children, and I needed some dinnerware and lunchboxes for the kitchen. "Where are we going?" I asked her, confused. She had missed the turn to the mall, and where else would we be going? "No, we're ditching the mall," she laughed, "We're going out thrifting today." She smiled, turning into a smaller parking area. It wasn't too busy. In the front was a small store, windows decorated with small trinkets, a dolled-up manikin, and a staff member, I assumed, arranging a few household items for the display. Not your usual store, I thought.

And that's when I was first introduced to the world of thrifting. We ended up buying what we came for and more!

And at the time, money was a bit tight, yes. But in the end, it didn't matter (you'll understand why in a minute). If you've ever heard horrifying stories about buying second-hand items, shake them off. You'll be doing yourself a favor. I can vouch for it!

But, what exactly is thrifting? Well, simply said, it's when you shop at thrift stores, garage sales, flea markets, and online platforms for lightly used items at discounted prices. It's buying second-hand or previously owned goods for next to nothing.

But first, let's start with the question that might be confusing you right now. What does thrifting have to do with the environment?!

Mainly, it's all about keeping items that are still perfectly fine and usable out of the bins and dumps. Items are usually donated and later purchased. From there, they could either be reused or reinvented, the choice is entirely up to you. Once, for example, I scrolled upon a craft where old t-shirts were turned into bags. It's a perfect deal, where old shirts someone grew tired of or was tugging too tightly around their waist are now used to keep sunglasses, snacks, and things for that family outing to the beach, all at a low price!

Thrift stores, I would have to say, stop hundreds of items from wasting away with the other garbage, not to mention clogging up landfills. And when you donate to these stores, you're also ensuring that your old things live on through others. So the worms will have to stick to the leftovers for now!

Thrifting is a simple, easy, and productive way to push for green! Disposing of unwanted waste takes a toll on the environment, as we know. Textile waste, such as clothing, is no exception and can take up to years to fully break down in landfills. So, when you buy and support second-hand clothing, you'll be helping the environment by cleaning up textile waste while also conserving energy and saving water. How? A lot goes into making clothing. For example, it takes more than 400 gallons of water to produce a single cotton t-shirt, and that's not to mention the chemicals used. And the same goes for all things we simply throw away, things that could still be used or have a second chance to be something new.

Today, we live in a world, a culture of the latest, greatest of fashion, electronics, and household items. Many things are bought, and as the trends sway, things are replaced. This is when opportunity steps in, allowing us to use these unwanted things and keep them from ending up in landfills.

The great thing is that these items aren't limited to trends, popularity, or market value. These are donated, pre-loved items of all kinds, with marks reflecting the good, bad, ugly, beautiful, and fashionable styles of every decade, telling all the stories they've witnessed. So, if you're looking for something one-of-a-kind, drop in at the thrift shop on the corner and browse through the used options. If you're patient, you could find things you wouldn't see anywhere else. This is also the case for rare and discontinued items, and sometimes you might find a literal treasure! We've all heard stories of the lost Picasso or Rembrandt some lucky thrifter stumbled upon at the junk store or flea market. You just never know!

On the other hand, if you're looking for clothes alone, you'll definitely get a spunky, chic, one-of-a-kind wardrobe at second-hand stores. These shops have a more unique, diverse assortment of clothing, meaning that you'll most likely not be bumping into someone else wearing the same sweater as you! (Though you might have a run in with the previous owner, who will adore your fashion sense, by the way!) You can also experiment with all the different styles that a thrift shop has to offer. Perhaps you're feeling a bit experimental, vintage, or ostentatious?

And another benefit is that if you dig through the racks, you could possibly stumble upon some quality brands at a steep discount. And because these stores get their things from donations, there will always be a more diverse, ever-changing selection to choose from weekly. This isn't just the case with clothing. There's nothing quite like the thrill of finding a great bargain, and these stores are overflowing with discounts for decor, appliances, equipment, you name it!

Quite frankly, people usually donate items that are gently used or essentially new. I've even found goods that still had their original tags attached! Most items, you see, are given away because people no longer feel they've got a use for them anymore. I've heard countless stories of people buying high-end goods that were in perfect condition for a great price. The previous owner simply didn't feel they needed the coffee machine anymore since the coffee shop sees them every morning. Most items were purchased with a purpose in mind, but then people simply realize that someone else would make better use of it. So, why not dodge the status price while glamming up your closet or home?

For me, the best thing about thrifting is the savings! It's a way to stretch your budget, which is especially useful in those months where your finances are a bit short. I mean, why pay more when there are cheaper alternatives out there, when you can buy the same, or similar, stuff you're looking for at a fraction of the cost?

One morning, my wife and I decided that it was about time we organized and packed up our belongings. We were thinking of setting up roots elsewhere, but that morning it was final. We wanted to put all the knick-knacks, clothes, kitchenware, and other small household items in big plastic storage boxes. We didn't want to buy them new, especially since we would need many of them for the move, and they retail for about $10 a box. So, we jumped onto Facebook Marketplace to look through all the options. Then we found it: the perfect listing, 11 of these containers for only $15. They only needed some dust wiped off, so it was a real steal!

It's a literal life-saver where you could also have some money left on the side for other expenses, a treat, or some other goals you've been saving for. And, you'll be living greener by helping the environment and having a greener wallet at the same time.

But no one wants to pay for something that breaks within a month or a day even! And I think that this is the dilemma many people are thrown into. We still want quality, or else we wouldn't be saving money anyway. You'll end up buying six to seven of the same item because it simply wears out, breaks, and doesn't last. But the key to thrifting is knowing the ins and outs of buying second-hand goods, which I'll be sharing with you later on. You have to identify what you're looking for, or because you don't need a shopping list in these stores, whether you could and will use the things you find.

It's a matter of grasping what you *shouldn't* get and evaluating the quality and condition of the products you want. By doing so, you could steal a great buy! Remember what I've said so far: second-hand goods don't mean cheap or mediocre things; it simply implies that someone else had owned it before you and they've chosen to part with it.

And a lot of these places, like thrift shops, flea markets, garage sales, and auctions, are scattered with hidden gems, like valuable paintings, jewelry, and tiny treasures the donor might not have noticed. Unlike department stores and boutiques where everything is folded, grouped, and labeled, these stores are places where you've really got to search for what you're looking for. And digging through these ruins of racks honestly feels like you're Indiana Jones on a quest for the best buys you can find! And please, don't feel bad when you buy these sort of rare items. As the saying goes: one man's trash is another man's treasure, after all.

It's also an opportunity and chance for you to take a stroll down memory lane, to remember things from your childhood or some other memories you're fond of, with goods like a Care Bear steel lunchbox or a He-Man action figure. Second-hand stores are usually filled with all sorts of vintage or collector items that will also spark some feelings or reminiscence from you.

And in time of need, these sales could be just what *you* need! We've all had those "I have nothing to wear" or "I could've sworn I put it there" moments. And with no luck or a memory lapse, you're left pulling your hair out about what you're going to do about that special occasion, job, or event or item you need. Running down to your local thrift shop can be of exceptional support in finding what you need quickly without spending hundreds on a new set of cutlery, elaborate attire, or considered gifts.

Or perhaps you're the host, and while you're getting everything ready you realize that you're short on platters and bowls, or you need a tool here and a small appliance there. You can't ask Joey, your neighbor, because he's convinced you've still got his French skillet from the last time your parents came to visit. You don't, or perhaps you do; either way, asking him is out of the question. And spending massive amounts of money on platters, appliances, or plates is futile, especially if you plan on rarely, or never, using it again in the future.

Your best bet would be to pop in at your local thrift shop to pick up everything needed without declaring bankruptcy at the end of it all. This will turn out a lot cheaper than you having to buy the same things brand new out of the box or having to rent it at a higher cost. And, when everything returns to normal, you could always donate it back to the shop or keep it around for next time, even lending it to Joey, perhaps!

Another way these more affordable prices could be of convenience is when we break away from our standard, everyday routines to go and enjoy the sun, beach, lodge, or wherever it might be. With the excitement of vacations and getting away, it's easy to forget some things you need when packing. Instead of going to the nearest store, look up a nearby thrift shop and make a trip down there. You could easily find what you need, like a comely dress for an unplanned dinner or swimming towels for the hotel pool. (But, if you've forgotten your toothbrush, I suggest you stick to buying it brand new.)

Also, when you're on vacation, it helps to look around these stores for unusual or out-of-season items that aren't available in the shops near you. Stores vary in what they have. An elderly person from Pretoria, for example, would be donating different things than that of a young adult from

California. So, browsing around in other stores in varying locations will give you a brand new feel and experience. That's the beauty of it!

Now, are you a parent or grandparent? Kids grow up so fast, don't they? And buying shirts, pants, and shoes every month while they do could be very costly and strenuous on your wallet. So, instead, bring them along to the shop to pick out more clothing for less and, in the meantime, you'll be teaching them a valuable lesson in shopping smart and sustainably by saving money with cheaper, pre-owned, yet still, quality clothing.

And both of you can actually be thrilled about the trip, because let's face it, tagging along with them to that new-trendy outlet, and thinking *I will never fit into those jeans again*, isn't fun. And they feel the same way when dragged to our favorite establishments, where there's nothing for them to look at. But, with thrifting, there's something for every generation. And when you're shopping for clothes, they could always peek in at the games, music, or entertainment sections. They won't get bored and beg you to hurry up, meaning that you could shop in peace.

But, if you're still young on the scene of adulthood, don't stress. Thrift stores are the perfect place for you to shop and furnish your very first place, even when your funds are leaving your hands tied. You could start small, buying the best your budget allows and upgrading pieces as you go. Or you could buy your things in slices from paycheck to paycheck, like starting with the bed base and headboard, and then the next time getting a mirror, drawer, or bedside table. Soon you'll have your place fully furnished and decorated the way you want!

There's also a fabulous opportunity for you to spice up your income, no matter your age when shopping at second-hand stores. They could be the perfect suppliers for you to buy bargain items and then resell them online or in person. It's simple and won't take up a lot of your time if you want to resell for a second income. You buy the item and do some repairs and restores if needed before adding it to your digital shelves for advertisement. From there, all you have to do is wait for a buyer and convince them to buy from you. You'll have some extra dough in your pocket in no time!

And you could always jazz up your home or create new things to sell with some creativity, fabrics, and beads! If you're wondering what you could do and use for your next DIY project, wonder no more! You can find all the basics and what you need right there at the store. Many pieces, like a closet, just need some tweaking, and in a matter of no time, you and some TLC could do the job!

And most importantly, you'll be lending a helping hand in supporting charitable causes. Many thrift shops, you see, are operated by non-profitable organizations, like churches, hospitals, and private schools. And, of course, donating your used goods will significantly support their cause and give your unwanted things a second chance in someone else's life. But, shopping at them is another sizable way for you to shoulder and help fund their aims and make a change. It's a chance to support and give back to your community.

But, with that said, keep in mind that there are second-hand shops out there selling to make a profit, simply selling used goods at prices that are, quite frankly, not that cheap. Yes, many of these profitable organizations are still involved with local charities but not all of them. These profit-stores do, however, prevent perfectly usable items from ending up in the dumps. And many people are given jobs and a paycheck.

My advice is to stick to charitable stores. Unlike big retail chains, thrifting stores are usually lone wolves existing for their customers and supporting local charities. Choosing to shop at your local thrift store driven to help others is a great way to help and support those who need it.

But, second-hand stores are often viewed as dumping grounds for things that are on their last legs: a quick fix to chuck all the unwanted, run-down goods. These stores are then saddled with rubbish that costs them a lot of money and time to get rid of, undermining their charitable intentions. You may feel good that you're 'recycling,' but it doesn't do anyone any good if what you're 'donating' is broken or soiled. So, be sensible. Are your things still donatable and usable? If not, find alternatives. If your clothes are a bit of a reversed ugly-duckling, give them a wash and cut them up—they make the perfect rags! And textile waste can be recycled just like plastic, although it still has a long way to go before it's a household name.

THE TIP-OFF ON THRIFTING

Thrift shopping is an essential step to making our world a greener place. It will teach and inspire others to do the same. But, if you're new to thrifting, it could be intimidating at times. It's a new scene you're stepping into, and you'll have to get used to how it works, what to do, and what not to get. You'll catch on quickly! But I'll start you off with a few quick tips and tricks I've learned over the years!

Know Why You're There

Thrifting without knowing why is a recipe for disaster. Have you ever gone grocery shopping on an empty stomach? Well, shopping blind is doing just that. It's doable, yes, but not ideal. You'll end up picking one item, then another, and another, and before you know it, you've overspent, and your budget is done.

And I don't mean that you should have a detailed shopping list in hand. You could, of course, write down if you're looking for something specific, but doing so isn't necessary. By knowing why you're thrifting, I mean that you should have a clear goal of why you're going. Do you need supplies for your crafts? Dishes and utensils for the kitchen? Are you on the hunt for the newest addition to your unique collection of old movie posters? Whatever your goal may be, it simply helps you narrow down what you're after.

If you want to focus on the kitchen, for example, you'll only be looking at kitchen-related items and not get distracted by all the other things there. It helps you stick to your budget, avoid overspending, and not regret any impulsive buys you might make.

A great idea would be to keep pictures, ideas, and inspirations on your phone to show to the clerk. She could advise or show you where to look in the store and whether they even have similar ideas for you to look at that are available.

Having an objective for when you go thrifting is a hack, one of those ins and outs of thrifting that could help you stay focused on what's in your cart while you're in a place filled with many options that could easily distract anyone.

Carrying Cash

Another way for you to stay on budget is to stick to cash when you go thrifting. Also, remember to stay with style and taste: don't purchase something on the plain fact that it's a name brand not pricey. If you aren't going to wear it, or it will end up in a box somewhere because it's not what you usually get, you probably shouldn't buy it. So, always ask yourself whether it's you and if you'd use it later on.

Out-Standing

Going through multiple piles, racks, shelves, and stacks of items is a lot of work, not to mention the time that will be wasted. Tackling all the things inside of these second-hand stores isn't for the faint at heart. Even though the size of these stores will vary, it doesn't matter. Learn how to master scanning through everything without missing any potential gems. Make your way through the store and scan around, pulling out the items that stand out for you. It does take focus and patience because it's a skill that will only develop over time.

Another important thing is to inspect every item you want to buy. Don't feel like you have to rush. Take the time to go over your finds before heading over to pay. It's easy to miss a small hole, tear, or stain, so it's better to pay attention to what's in your shopping pile to save yourself from the heartbreak of finding these defects too late.

Some Friendly Advice

Once you've found the thrift shop for you, start making friends with the staff there. They can help, guide, and advise you on your purchases, which is especially useful when you're still getting used to everything. And why not make more friends who could help you out? Also, try and share your personal experiences with others, your friends, family, and colleagues. At first, I was doubtful about buying second-hand things, but it's vital in reducing waste caused by discarded goods. We have to motivate others to give it a shot because we have to keep these things from ending up with the garbage while we're still in the midst of our trash crisis.

The No-Zones for Buying Used Goods

There are, however, things you might not want to buy second-hand, most of which might risk your health. So, to be safe, purchase these items new. Yes, all products are cleaned, but we can't know all the shops and sellers, so it's better to be safe than sorry.

- Underwear and swimwear
- Hats and helmets
- Some shoes
- Mattress
- Older models that aren't much cheaper than the newer models
- Some obsolete technology isn't worth it, like old TV's, but if it means something to you, then it's fine to buy
- Items that will cost you a lot to repair, unless it's of importance to you
- Toothbrushes and gum guards
- Piercings
- Basically, things that goes inside of your body are a no-go

Digital Deals

As we all know, the world is going digital, and with that, it means that various online second-hand sites are popping up, which provides you with a more convenient way of finding pre-owned or refurbished items. You'll also be presented with many more options in one place, instead of having to go shop to shop until you find the right thing for you. It's really an easy process that you might find works great for you.

First of all, I would suggest hunting around on Facebook Marketplace for what you want. Look at all the different choices, paying close attention to the price, condition, description, and sometimes, even at the seller's reviews and previous listings, if they have any, to make sure that they're reliable. There are a lot of fakes and con artists out there, and online shops have made it a breeze for more scammers and thieves to emerge with much more comfort and ease. So, the best shot to dodge these scams and time-wasters is to stay focused, look and observe closely, identify red flags, and trust your gut! And *never* go to someone's home to pick something up if you don't know them. Meet in a public place or tag a friend along.

But don't let that scare you off. Not all sellers are tricksters who want to steal your money from right under you! Many of them simply want to make an income by selling their things in a more spacious, digitized store!

However, possible scams aren't the only problem. You can't, for example, hold the product in front of you to see if there are any dents, holes, or condition faults, or try it on if it's clothing. And sometimes, you could buy something that doesn't work at all. You'll have to trust what the buyer and the pictures are telling you or see if they have a return policy. It's a system where your trust is tested, and sometimes, sadly, you were right to be suspicious. But then again, other times you receive just what you wanted, neatly packaged, in excellent, working condition. It's a gamble, yes, but sometimes you've got to have a little faith!

Another thing you've got to consider before sealing the deal is the location of the listing. If it's too far and the drive isn't worth it, you might have to continue looking elsewhere. Or you could always ask the seller whether the product could be couriered to you. Just make sure to use an eco-friendly courier service and that you don't overspend on the delivery costs. If the shipping costs leave you drowning in expenses, leave it. Preferably, go browse around on other platforms, like Instagram or eBay, to see whether there are better options for you there.

By this time, you either find the perfect listing for you and make arrangements to snatch up your buy. Or you've still got some platforms to explore. Your next step would be to ask around for possible options to go check out. Or go search in second-hand stores (the physical ones) to see what they have to offer and what's on sale, focusing on searching for the item you're looking for.

And then, if all else fails, I would have to say that you should continue your search longer. Sometimes finding the perfect listing can take some time, months, and years even. So, if you're patient and you have the time to wait, keep repeating the process. But if you don't, I would suggest you look around for the most affordable deal you can get buying the item new.

We all should consider at least trying to buy at second-hand stores, but when all is said and done, buying to save or make money, supporting charities, or wanting to help the environment are all clever choices to make. It still remains your choice, however, and if you give it a try and it doesn't work out for you, it's fine! Yes, it's really a great way to reduce waste, but it's not the end of the world if you choose otherwise. You gave it a try, and that's what counts. You could always try later in life. And nothing is stopping you from donating!

Change is a complex matter, and it comes in many shapes and forms. You don't have to do it all to make a difference. Doing one thing at a time is already a great move in the right direction of going green.

6

YOUR CARBON FOOTPRINT

I don't have a carbon footprint, because I ...

DRIVE EVERYWHERE

Have you ever seen yourself driving down the streets, like James Dean, but without the roaring of a loud engine spurting out clouds of smoke? Well then, maybe it's the perfect time to hop into an electric vehicle (EV) of your own!

These cars are becoming more mainstream, but if you're still on the fence about snatching yourself an electric, don't worry, you're not the only one. So, how can I convince you otherwise? Well, by one again giving you all the reasons why electric is the way to go. Yes, you'll be saving money, but green travel is by far the biggest brag these cars have, in my opinion.

Electric cars are also just hugs to the environment, as you might have guessed by its presence in the chapter. These cars come with zero tailpipe emissions, meaning that we could be looking forward to cleaner air in no time. And as you know, cleaner air means healthier people and fewer diseases, less stress on public health systems like hospitals, and so on. Our carbon footprint will reduce dramatically. You'll also press MUTE on noise pollution due to the quietness of electric cars both inside and outside of the vehicle. Maybe you'll be able to hear the birds chirping in Los Angeles after all!

Now, a lot of people are worried about the price tag. The costs of EVs can vary, some being expensive, while some work out cheaper than your traditional gas vehicles. EVs also cost significantly less to run and maintain than gas-powered cars. There will no longer be any oil changes, smog tests, and fewer repairs on your moving parts that break and wear out. Plenty of electric car owners even claim that they could go years without any repair or service bills.

But that doesn't mean you're getting off easy, sadly. You should still keep a good eye on your breaks, although they'll still last longer than that of gas-powered vehicles. But, I would say that your biggest issue comes with your battery. Still, today, most models come with an 8-year/100,000-mile warranty, and they're expected to last for about 15 years in a mild climate, so either way, your luck is looking up!

Just remember that when your battery has seen its last ride, dispose of it properly! The ideal would be direct recycling. It's a promising method for manufacturing sustainability. First, workers would vacuum away the electrolytes and shred battery cells. Then, the binders are removed with heat or solvents. And finally, a flotation technique is used to remove anode and cathode materials. This process is still quite a fixer-upper. But with the rapidly changing battery market, the future looks promising.

Electric cars are also absolutely comfortable performance cars that are a pleasure to drive. And in some states, you could be eligible for a significant rebate or credit on your taxes simply for choosing to go electric. But this is not a promise. Some states may offer less, nothing, or may tack on a little extra. There's also talk of special rate plans and rebates that will make your entry into EV easier. This is due to an increased urgency of incentivizing off-peak charging, considering the majority of EV charging occurs at home, meaning you can give the gas station a skip at last!

Electric cars are the future of transportation where you'll not only be seen as the Schumacher's of the road, but you'll be making a difference for the environment. While encouraging greener travel, you'll also have the chance to pack away some money for yourself. With the evolution of these vehicles, the choice will be easier for you to make. And all the cons will fall on deaf ears!

But, woah, reverse that. What disadvantages are we talking about?

High costs, limited range, performance problems, longer charge time … but the price and performance we've already established has been and will become better very soon. In the same way that computers and mobile phones became less expensive and more efficient as they evolved, so too with EVs. All of these other disadvantages are and will improve over time. Already more and more communities are providing charging stations, and the mileage efficiency of these cars is constantly improving.

Types of Electric Vehicles

- Battery Electric Vehicles (BEVs): These vehicles are powered by an electric battery, without any gas engine parts.
- Hybrid Electric Vehicles (HEVs): This is a low-

emission vehicle that uses an electric motor to assist gas-powered engines. Power comes from gas and cannot be charged.

- Plug-in Hybrid Electric Vehicles (PHEVs): This is the same as a hybrid, but it has a larger battery and electric motor. It still has its gas tank but could charge.

Alternatively, grab your running shoes, bicycle helmet, jump on a train, bus, or tag along with a friend. These ways of travel will definitely kick down your carbon footprint!

THE GREEN CABIN

We've already discussed how herds of people have stomped together, sharing awareness of how we should live with the planet in mind. The majority of us have accepted the basics of doing just that. Without ever giving it a second thought, recycling and composting our rubbish has become the norm in many households. Don't get me wrong, this is fantastic news! And these two lifestyle choices are still employed as our essential helpers, which is why I included them.

But, the basis of pushing a greener life over the edge, for me, would be to ensure that your so-called habitat is sustainable, environmentally respectful, and efficient.

But how do you go about paying the piper without ending up broke at the end of it all? That's the fear, isn't it? The price tag of converting a traditionally built home into one that is more eco-acceptable can often be more than we think we can afford.

I've got some news for you: eco-homes don't always mean diving between couches for some spare change and taking out hundreds of dollars from your savings. Quick recap: small changes are the way to go! You don't have to go all out right away, or at all even.

I kicked it all off by replacing the incandescent bulbs in my home with LED lights whenever they burned out. It was a modest shift, yes, but soon my entire house was lit up with LEDs, even the Christmas lights! I have since saved up a lot of energy and money since I no longer had to run to the store for replacements as much as I used to. These bulbs are also not as hot or hazardous as your standard, everyday bulbs. Energy-saving light bulbs, I can assure you, are the way to go, to step closer to shielding the environment. They may appear more expensive at first, but they burn so much more efficiently and last so much longer, they really do save you money in the long run.

What are other ways to go about eco-ing up your homestead? Well, a great way to reduce your carbon footprint is by being a warrior about your choices regarding the cooling and heating of your home.

Air conditioning and heating are standard household luxuries. But they steal loads of energy and it takes a sweeping blow at the environment. It's not worth it. But, some places in the world are more temperate than others, and cooling down the home could, in some cases, be necessary: for example, if you have indoor animals who could die from the heat. Or maybe you're just not ready to part away with the breeziness it offers during those torrid summer days. This is also fine. No one likes to feel as though they're a lobster boiling in a pot!

Just make sure you're making intelligent shopping decisions. For air conditioning, you have two options to pick from: a split system and a packaged central air conditioning system (which is quite a mouthful to say, I know). Split systems have outdoor cabinets that compress and condense air, spurting the hot air outside. The packaged central system uses ducts to worm through walls or your roof to connect to the air conditioner that's outside. Whichever one you decide to go for, both will do the job, all while lowering your bills, energy use, carbon footprint, and environmental damage. So, you can't go wrong with either one.

As for heating, there are a few options to choose from, all of them working towards helping you bend the temperatures to your desire.

Insulating your home is a great place to start if you want warmth but not the excessive energy use that comes with it. It's also a brilliant way to set aside some money for a rainy day. Your walls and roof are the easiest way to go about it, but another great way to grab onto as much heat as you can could be to look at your windows as insolation too. I'm talking about double-glazing, which is when your windows have two sheets of glass enclosing a sealed air space. It looks like a very tiny alleyway between building-walls of glass … if you were an ant, that is.

These double-pane windows work by keeping cold air out in the winters and warm heat out in the summers, making it a downright double threat! And as with most eco-friendly alternatives, you'll be dropping down on your energy costs and saving money in the long run. However, I won't lie. Savings are in the long run because the initial costs, according to a specialized company, could range anywhere from $2,800 to $4,700. This all depends on how many windows you have, their sizes, and the window style you're aiming for. But, sometimes, your location could mean lower prices, and you never know. You might find a deal somewhere along the road, and sometimes you can get a tax break for the investment.

Some tips I would advise you to follow would be to invest in wooden window frames, because even when glazing is a boon for saving energy, the UPVC window surroundings can be very polluting as they release toxic compounds. These wooden frames are more eco-friendly, and with some proper care, could be just as durable and hard-working as any other.

And with or without double-glazed windows, ditch the blinds and preferably go for some thick, luscious curtains. They can be great energy conservers and, in the summers, when pulled shut, they can help keep rooms cooler.

Another option you can shoot for is underfloor heating, which is what it sounds like: heating under your floors. It does, however, follow the same reversed gains as double-glazed windows, where you have to spend some money to save some money. The initial cost could be considerable, not to mention the upheaval in your house due to the installation.

And while we're on the floor, I think it's the perfect time to bring up the materials you choose for them. Sustainable flooring made from recycled materials, such as bamboo hardwood, cork, carpet tiles, and natural linoleum are a simple yet effective carbon footprint reducer. And because these renewable materials lack volatile organic compounds (gas emitted from certain solids or liquids, like adhesives and paints, that are very common in our homes), they end up improving air quality.

But there are also more ways you could give your house a more aesthetically pleasing look and feel, like using water-based paints on your walls. Your ordinary paints are usually oil-based, meaning that they're not as eco-friendly as they could be. Water-based, in contrast, contains natural pigments that, for some, even offer a nicer variety of colors.

With the 21st century providing us with more innovative, greener inventions and tweaks to existing ones, a certain one sparked my eco-interest. A clever way to regulate your home's temperature is using meters.

Now, there are two types of these meters. One is a thermostat that offers ultimate control over the temperature of your home. It also allows you to choose energy-saving settings, pitches you tips on saving energy, and has features to monitor your energy consumption. The other one, the smart meter, could be programmed to turn on at certain times during the day so that you could, for example, come home to a cozy house after work.

Often these meters are confused as the same thing, but they're not. The main difference between them is that the thermostat gives you remote control over your heating system. The smart meter, on the other hand, deals with all your gas and electricity readings. Either way, they're real eye-openers that monitor and cap your electricity use.

And now, the water-saving solutions. First up, as we step into the bathroom, we look at a water-saving toilet. This is known as a low-flow toilet that effectively decreases your water use. It uses about 1.9 to 5.4 gallons less when you flush than your standard flusher. But how? it extracts less water from local pipes, thus using as little water as possible. The same concept applies to your low-flow showerheads, which pause a running shower once it gets warm until you're ready to hop in. According to the EPA, just doing that could save an average family around 2,900 gallons of water in a year. Also, if you happen to stumble upon a WaterSense label smacked onto a faucet while you're browsing in the store, know that it means that the faucet is 20% more water-efficient than other faucets. They could be used in the kitchen or in the bath, or in both!

Not only will these strategic moves have an impact on your water preservation, but you'll notice a tremendous difference in next month's water bill!

Some of these changes might turn out costly, but for now, just cross out those that you're not prepared to spend lots on, focusing on those you're left with, and always look up new ways you could make your house more eco-friendly.

But, if you happen to have some money lying around, you're willing to save up or take out a loan, the option would be to look at some Energy Star appliances and solar panels, which is something I've been 'burning' to get off my chest.

A POCKET FULL OF SUNSHINE

Solar is a revolutionary energy solution, yet whenever I would bring up solar energy around the office, people would grunt and roll their eyes with a great sigh. One day, after just such a reaction, I decided to ask them why that is. My colleagues told me that the mere mention of solar panels brought up pictures of spammy ads that promised free panels or installation. Or of those steadfast salesmen who wouldn't take 'no' for an answer even after they had basically begged him to accept that it wasn't possible for them at the time.

That's why I'm promising that this isn't the case. I'm not here to sell you products or services. My goal has been and continues to be very simple: to lay down all the facts with an opinion or two (or a really bad pun) slipped in between. And in this case, to break the myths and lay out the pros and cons of investing in solar energy.

Solar Squad

Apart from upping your home's value, as mentioned, the uppermost benefit of solar energy is pretty straightforward. You're generating your own power using the sun as your battery. Slowly, you'll become less dependent on electricity bills, sometimes eliminating them altogether. Solar energy could cut your electricity bills by decades, considering its lifespan is typically 25 to 35 years. You'll be laughing all the way to the bank in no time!

And because the energy is clean and renewable, your carbon emissions and environmental impact would diminish, even topping the ranks in terms of being the best eco-friendly solution.

What about the anxiety of those rising utility electricity bills? Wave goodbye to that! Going solar puts you in the cockpit when it comes to the generation of energy. Within a decade, the cost of electricity has risen about 5%, and it's only expected to spike more, whereas solar energy has shown a drop of nearly 70% within the same timeframe. This means that it's even less expensive to install solar now than it was 10 years ago.

With the rise of interest in renewable energy sources comes the increase of goals to reduce greenhouse gas emissions, which means there's no better time to come aboard. Also, there have been budding incentives on the rise that could help your rope in all your investments.

Solar renewable energy credits and net-metering are examples of two key benefits that allow you to earn credit or cash on your bills. This is to compensate you for the electricity generated by your solar panels. So, cross your fingers and hope that you're in one of those states where these incentives are applied because you could be expecting both immediate and long-term returns.

A No-Go

With the good comes the bad, which means we'll have to do your research when looking at the disadvantages. Before getting your hopes up, you should know that solar panels don't work for every roof.

Many solar panels are mounted to your roof. The problem comes with certain older roofing materials, such as slate and cedar tiles, and rooftop additions like skylights and roof decks, all of which could make the solar array installation difficult or costly. But if your home doesn't qualify for roof mounting or your house is lacking enough sunshine (usually a minimum amount of sun exposure is required), it's not the end of the world. You do still have options, such as mounting the solar panels to the ground, or you could buy a share in a community shared garden.

But, if you're planning on moving soon, it simply won't be ideal. Yes, these systems are great investments, but it could take some time before it breaks even. As you know, installing panels could improve your property value and thus increase your return when you decide to sell your house. So, all of these benefits will be lost unless you buy the system with cash. But you see, not everyone has that sort of moola on hand, and the cost could be intimidating.

That being said, there are various solar financing options out there. Using, for example, power purchase agreements and state-backed loans could help you get around the problem. But even after doing all that, another problem jumps to mind: finding local installers of quality and comparing their quotes. Solar power is a fast-growing market that waits for no one, and everyone is out with plates for a slice of the cake!

But, I'll give you some advice. There are more convenient ways to shop around for your best deal, an easier way that puts you, the homeowner, in control. So, what is it? Using online comparison-shopping platforms, like EnergySage Solar Marketplace, to grab onto and compare solar quotes from the top installers in your area.

How Does Solar Work, Anyway?

Solar power is a complex process, but the short answer would be that solar cells, made from silicon, are a semiconductor that can generate electricity. This entire process is known as the *photovoltaic effect*.

These photovoltaic cells absorb the sun's energy, converting it to DC electricity. From there, the electricity is converted to AC electricity, which most home appliances use. The electricity flows throughout your home, powering your electronic devices as the electricity powered by your solar panels is fed to the electric grid.

But then again, there's also alternative solar tech out there, such as solar hot water and concentrated solar power. The latter transforms sunlight into heat. With concentrated solar power installation, mirrors reflect the sun to a focal point that collects and stores heat energy to help provide power to an electricity grid. Solar hot water systems work, more or less, with the same concept. These systems capture thermal energy from the sun to produce heat, heating the water for your home.

A FAQ: Can You Run Your Whole House on Solar Power?

Yes, you can generate enough electricity to power your entire house. All you have to do is ensure that everything is working at its best by choosing the right type of panels, installer, and the best angle for your home to absorb the most rays.

However, expecting that level of production every day is not realistic. The weather is not a constant promise: we do sometimes have dark clouds and rain. But, you can install storage to help if you don't want to rely on the grid when the sun isn't out.

CHANGE STARTS WITHIN

*id you hear about the nun who delayed doing her laundry? She had a ...*

FILTHY HABIT

Food, water, toys, cars, furniture, clothing, knick-knacks, and other goods. We all know that we're an immense population thriving on our need to consume. But we've come to realize our prior mistakes and we've taken responsibility for our actions, knowing that we have to if we don't want to lose our future.

But going green isn't as simple as stopping our consumption completely. It would be impossible to halt every single thing we're doing. We'll always need to take and pick from our surroundings to survive as a species, it's inevitable. The key, however, is in developing higher mindfulness of our consumption habits and taking on newer, better, and more sustainable ones instead.

I studied business for 8 years before working for various organizations. What I've noticed and learned over the years was that all of them had differing business strategies and ways of doing things. With this knowledge, I've steered my focus toward building my very own start-up. Throughout my career, whether it was working for the big man or running my own company, and in my life in general, one fundamental factor never changed. You see, there's importance and influence in the habits we have; they shape, sculpt, and frame how we do things. There's a power in what we believe is the norm and what we accept as routine.

If we were to make a habit of throwing wrappers in the park every day, soon the grass would be a junkyard of papers. But, if we were to turn it all around and make a habit out of reversing our actions, instead, picking up those candy leftovers, we would have a clean park where the grass, plants, and trees would grow. And animals could live without mistaking Snicker-wrappers for a branch! By changing our habits, we would learn to live with the environment in mind; it would come as second nature without you even having to think about it.

It's not an easy thing to do, however. You won't break your environmentally damaging habits simply by saying, "Well, I don't want to do that anymore!" although deciding to stop is always a great place to start. The process will take some good amount of time, as well as consistent, conscious efforts to both get rid of the old and take on the new.

I'm sure you've heard that you only need to tough it out for 21 days: after that, your habits are broken, and new ones can be programmed. For some people, yes, this could be the case. But, the truth is, there really is no hard-and-fast time frame for breaking and forming habits. Various personal factors come into play, like how long you've had the habit, what rewards you get from it, or whether it's fully integrated into your life.

A rough answer, but a more realistic estimate of how long habit formation would take is around 10 weeks for most people. But studies say that this too is not a set-in-stone time frame. It could honestly take 18 days, or anywhere from 8 months and up. You have to understand that it's not a sprint. It's a process that will leave you drenched in sweat. It demands patience and an understanding that when you're eliminating these habits, you're helping the environment, and slowly strolling towards an improved life overjoyed with more sustainable customs.

HACKING AWAY AT HABITS

People often try to take on more than they can chew. You could doom yourself for failure if you attempt to break several habits all at once. I know we all want to do as much as we can to help the environment. But what if you feel that you have bad habits when it comes to saving water and electricity, you've got a problem with waste, or you're just not the best at keeping things as green as they could be? It would be chaos to take on everything from the get-go. Sometimes the approach does work, yes, but it's better to be safe than sorry. You don't want to do so much that you feel overwhelmed and discouraged. Instead, take it stone by stone until you reach your mile-rock!

You could, for example, start with your water habits before you jump over to being more mindful of your electricity use. If you're watering your garden daily, cut back to only once or twice a week as needed. Then, you could cut back on your screen time and learn to do more things outside or without power, like creating recycled trinkets or cleaning up the park.

So, I would lock in on a habit or an area of the environment you want to focus on. If you're lacking in more than one (or you're unsure, or it's small habits here and there), single them out! Take on one by one until you're a whiz when it comes to living sustainably with routines that are the envy of your neighbors!

It's just a better way to go about it, honestly. It doesn't help anyone if you're feeling overwhelmed and flooded by everything you've put on your shoulders. Work on taking one turn at a time and dropping habits bit by bit. There are more benefits in small, progressive goals anyway!

And don't be alarmed if you catch yourself slipping every now and then, or you keep repeating the behavior you want to stop. It happens! Accept the setback and move on. Instead, swap this over to your advantage, use your slip-ups to grow, and accept these new, fresh habits until they're almost reflex-like, and you're doing them unintentionally.

Identify how you slipped: were you distracted with work? On the phone? Or did you simply just forget? And then map out ideas and ways to prevent it from happening in the future. Let's say you've just taken on recycling, and you're so used to throwing things in one bin that you can't help but do it. Well, stick post-its all over the kitchen! And superglue lids onto the bins to demand your attention to it if you have to! (A bit extreme, yes, and impractical, but I hope you get the point.) Just find techniques that work for you and assist you in achieving your goals.

And the ultimate way is to genuinely *want* it. If not, the motivation, drive, and effort won't be there. Think about why you want to help the environment. Are you afraid of the future that will follow if you sit back? Is it so that your family could enjoy a brighter tomorrow when you're no longer around? Or are you simply passionate about the environment? Whatever your reasons are, let that move you towards better sustainable habits. And it also doesn't hurt to look at and remember the long-term benefits you'll gain by leaving behind all of these damaging habits. Everything will improve!

Letting go of some habits and taking on newer, sustainable ones have clear benefits. But, sometimes, it's hard for some people to see. And if you haven't quite put your finger on it, go sit down and talk it out with yourself until you have an answer. In this case, most of these habits are harmful to the environment, directly or indirectly. And you want to change because you want better for the planet, the people you love, and future generations to come. There are, of course, other reasons, but the reasons are personally yours!

So, when you know why you want to help the environment, let that ground you. This is no longer a maybe-or-maybe-not game (not that it ever was). We need to take action and do our part before it's too late, and this is how we can do just that. And before you know it, you've worked through your list of bad habits, and you're living a greener, more sustainable life!

SUSTAINABLE STYLES

Getting into the habit of eco-friendly living should become part of your weekly or even daily routine. While some of these habits are simple, they can be very beneficial in the long run. And as with all customs, it all starts at home!

Cutting Back on Adam's Ale

Water shortage and pollution, as we know, is one of the top problems we have to face. And quite frankly, there are many habits we can all learn to hold onto that will save considerable amounts of H_2O and clean up the lakes and oceans as we go along. By choosing to conserve water now, we'll not only clean up our lakes and oceans, but we'll secure clean, drinkable, and accessible water for the future.

So, let's head over to the bathroom first. The primary habit to kick, apart from not flushing unnecessarily, is not to leave the water running while you're brushing your teeth, washing your hands, or shaving. Open the tap, close it, do your thing, and open it up again to finish up. This small action could save up to 4 gallons per person: for example, if you're a part of a household of four, brushing twice a day adds up to about 32 gallons!

It goes to show how unaware we are of the amount of water we waste doing everyday things. Take showering. Not many people are conscious of how long their showering sessions last. Do you know? On your typical day, the average shower is around 8 minutes, with about 2.5 gallons of water used per minute—that's 20 gallons a shower! But, when you cut down the time you're in there to about 5 minutes, you could be saving at least 7.5 gallons. And, I know! Shower time, for many people, is a time and space where they can daydream, perform, sing, and relax, but sometimes you've got to make some sacrifices and cut the show short!

We still have some time though, so let's stay in the shower for a second. From the previous chapter's low-flow showerhead to scrubbing quicker than Usain Bolt, taking a shower is still better than taking a bath.

But, if you prefer the tub, or it's your only option, remember not to pull the plug on the water. Grab a bucket and start scooping. The same goes for any other water you don't finish, like filling a glass of water to drink and not finishing it, or while you're waiting for the warm water from the faucet so you can do the dishes.

Use your recycled water for your plants, unless there are chemicals or residues in the water that could harm your greenery. Or you could clean your driveway after sweeping it clean with a broom to get rid of the harder stains, but leave the outdoor hosing out of it! You could also use the water to clean your car, floors, and whatever else you can think of, depending on the water's condition.

Also, remember to inspect and do maintenance on your pipes as much as possible to prevent leaks that could go unnoticed for years. And, while we're at it, insulating your hot water pipes is a great way to reduce wasting water while you're waiting for it to heat up.

Among other water-related habits, get used to piling up your laundry and dishes before popping them into their machines. Also, avoid defrosting food in warm water, rather keep to the fridge or cover and put it outside in the sun. Then, last but not least, choose tap water over bottled water to reduce the need for plastic. The main difference you can make is to only use water when you have to.

Nontoxic Homes

I've briefly discussed how you need to be using greener cleaning products. But the thing is, it's not only cleaning products that have made our indoor air more polluted than outdoor air. The habit lies in choosing eco-friendly, less-toxic cleaning products, detergents, fragrances, candles, body care, and more. Switching your products and paying attention to the ingredients before buying is, honestly, pivotal to ensuring that you and your family could live healthier inside of your home.

Eco-friendly products have never been more popular, but many shoppers don't know what they're actually buying. And I get it, companies have to make money too, as organic is the new market in town. But, still, I see their tricks and slips. So, it's up to you to see through all those labels to get the real story.

How To Know if It's Truly Green

- *What's in it?*
- Focus on the ingredients, looking at the shorter and more specific components. Consult online lists, databases, forums, apps, or other resources if you're unsure about anything.
- *Packaging*
- Prioritize glass, metal, and paper packaging, as you can recycle, reuse, or biodegrade them easier than other sorts of packaging, like plastic. (I know we're all used to 'recycling' plastic but the reality is, not all plastic is easily recyclable. Bottles, yes. Those clear clamshells? Not so much.)
- *Certification and logos*
- Many health or eco-friendly claims made by brands are verified by third parties with certifications that end up making the products look like giraffes with all those polka-dots. These cannot always be trusted if you don't know the source. However, looking these up on the internet is an option that works wonders!

Efficient Electricity

I know you're probably sick of me talking about turning off lights when you're not using them, but here we go again! I'll try and not repeat myself when it comes to these ways to reduce your electricity use. And I'll keep it short, with only three habits pitched below.

First, let your dishwasher breathe. This means that instead of running the drying cycle, aim for the air-dry option or open the door when you're off to bed for some zero-energy action. Second, the same goes for your dryer. Leave it out of this! Instead, dry your clothes on a rack or clothesline. And third, wash your clothes in cold water, which gets them just as clean with half the energy!

Green Beaches

Wherever you're headed, make sure that you make your trip as green as you possibly can! Before starting your travel, there are a few things you could do to make the take-off a bit smoother.

- *Packing light*: Sometimes flying is needed to get where you're going, especially if the destination is far away. Packing light could help the plane use less fuel, even if it's only by a little. Planes use the most fuel while taking off and landing, so the more they weigh, the more fuel they would use. You can also buy carbon offsets if you absolutely have to fly, which is a way of paying it forward by giving money to a company/charity that 'offsets' the carbon footprint you create by flying.
- *Green travel agent*: If you're not much of a planner, I feel you. You can always scan around for a green travel agent who can check on green certifications of hotels, tour guides, cruises, and so forth. They could

also often help you find unique places in nature if you wish to stay away from high-traffic tourist spots.

- *Green roofing*: Find a place to stay that has committed itself to sustainability. These places usually use water- and energy-efficient appliances and may wash sheets every few days. They could also have greywater systems, solar panels, and more. If you're with an agent, they could easily find the place to fit your needs. But, if you're on your own, I suggest that you look around on the internet for your best options. You can, for example, look at B&Bs from the Green Business Network or through Green Hotels Association until you find the perfect match!
- *Reusable containers*: Bring along your bags, bottles, food containers, and other items we sometimes 'buy when we get there.' Just because you're on vacation doesn't mean you have to ditch your container habits. But be sure that these containers are empty before you go through security at the airport to prevent any possible problems.
- *During the trip*: When you're there, instead of renting a car, use public transport, and if safe, walk, bike, or use carpool services, such as Uber, Bolt, and Lyft. Maybe you're interested in seeing places you might never have seen before, or hearing about the local history and culture? The best option would be to hire a local guide to assist you. They could possibly show you astounding hiking and biking trails, fine destinations, and rare spots. Also, remember to still eat locally as much as possible. You could also ask the local guide or accommodation owner for local shop recommendations.
- *When you're back home*: Going on vacation can be truly inspiring and motivational, especially if you

saw a part of the wilderness that shines its beauty. But soon, you'll get swept up back into our daily routine and schedules. So, to harness your inspiration, donate or volunteer at an organization before you get distracted.

More Little Habits

Once you start adopting these habits, soon they'll become a standard part of your lifestyle. My wife calls it my 'picnic basket,' although it's not really a basket at all. It's a small shoulder bag, where I store all the reusable things I bring to cafes, fast food joints, and restaurants. There's a cup, mug, Tupperware, cutlery, and a metal straw. All of which is a set of two each, just in case I break or forget to bring one.

I've been asked loads of times if I didn't find it strange or embarrassing to pull out my own kitchenware in front of all those people. And what must the staff think?!

Look, there's nothing wrong with wanting to reduce the amount of waste! People can stare if they like. I know why I'm doing what I'm doing, and even though, to some, I must look really silly, yes, I'm not ashamed. There's really no reason to be. As for the staff, I really hope I've never offended anyone because of it, but they are generally unphased by it. I'm still buying goodies from them, just on my plates and cups from my trunk. Nobody minds, really. And when we order in, we simply save up all the napkins and condiments in the cabinets and ask that they don't send along any plastic cutlery.

I also have a problem where, when I'm in the bathroom, for example, and get lazy, I might say I'll recycle the toilet roll 'later on.' Later on would come, and I've already forgotten. So my wife came up with a great idea. We got a separate set of recycling bins just for the bathroom. It works great on those lazy days, and there are no more toilet roll assemblies on the kitchen sink!

We also have the same concept in our kitchen: a separate bin that we use for our compost-on-the-go (well, not on the go exactly, just for when we're cooking). This way the eggshells go straight from my hands to where they belong. The same goes for the peels and other scraps.

From here on out, I mostly do all of the simple things, which I'm sure you've been called out for in the past: turning on the electronics and appliances and not heating or cooling a room when there's no one in it. As I said, start small, and that's what we did, but those small changes have stuck with us and they will too. As Allen F. Morgenstern said, "Work smarter, not harder!"

AFTERWORD

My aim has been to show you unique ways to reshape the ways we see and treat our planet. We want to help, that's all there is to it. We have aspired to face and understand what has been going on in the world, and what the future would look like if we were to continue down this path.

And now here we are: our time together comes to an end. We have walked together as the chapters came alive with life and our care for that life grew. We started off a bit dark, serious, and worried about the state our world was in. But, as we walked throughout the chapters and I shared my stories and bad jokes, I have found peace inside of me. It wasn't expected or planned, but it happened. I somehow know, hope, and believe that the world is safely looked after and that the future is not all doom and gloom after all. And I hope you feel that too.

We've talked through solutions, some of which we all wish we could do more of, and some miniature changes we could accept into our own lives to make a big change at the end of the day. We've learned some art and thrifting skills, and even ways to leave your wallet thicker.

But, what I've taken away as my main focus—and no, you don't have to agree with me, of course—is a feeling of when I was that passionate young boy again. The memories of a loving devotion toward the environment came back in a flash. And I can only hope you felt it too. Maybe you remembered the time you were in the park with your friends and you saw someone litter, and how that made you feel, so that you were driven to pick it up to keep your park clean? Or maybe when you were at home doing crafts with your mom or grandparent, and were enthralled that one common object like a bottle cap or cotton ball could be transformed into a Christmas tree ornament?

This is why I did it. It's why I wrote the book in the first place: to bring people back to a nostalgic time in their lives where the environment made them happy. Where they can appreciate all our planet has done for us and remember how they once treasured it.

But, sadly, as we grow up, many of us struggle to remember this, those precious times where everything seemed simpler and better. We forgot or we were too busy to care. Then, on the news and on television we see all of these things about global warming and climate change, and it sparks a remembrance in us. But, it's also overwhelming. We can't help but wonder, what can we do now? It seems so much bigger than just picking up trash or reusing a bit of plastic.

We now see countries, companies, communities, and individuals stepping up to the plate to help undo the wrong we have done. And I mention this because, sometimes, I have felt alone in this, and I know you have as well. But now we see that we aren't alone in this fight and that we can depend on others to raise their voice towards what is right; that together, as one, we can make a valuable change in this world.

In the start, we had no idea what to grasp and where to pull for a change, but I hope that you now have all the right tools and knowledge to take that giant leap forward. Your part in all of this is enormous and remarkably notable. Without you, the biodiversity we now know might one day end up as a mere footnote in the history books, if there's life after this at all.

So, do as much as you can! Live greener with the environment in mind. Recycle, up-cycle, reuse, reduce, refuse, compost, thrift, go eco-home, drive cleaner, and change your habits to live a better life. I mean, after all of this, I don't know how anyone wouldn't be convinced to do more to protect and restore our natural world.

Imagine a future where everything is fine. The Amazon rainforest is greener than ever. The Arctic is covered in thick slabs of ice. Our soil remains rich, and the wilderness reclaims its rightful place beside us. Take the coronavirus pandemic, for example, when the world moved indoors and everything grew quiet. Negative environmental human activity dropped, and with it, the wildlife came out of hiding. We sat in awe, even when they were found in the strangest of places. I mean, imagine stepping out of your apartment building or home and seeing foxes playing in the park! Or wolves walking down urban streets. Places they were avoiding, were now, once again, brimming with wildlife! Nature has a way of bouncing back if we let it. Imagine what can happen if we encourage it? This is a future we can have, where we could live in peace with the world around us, where we respect each other and nature, where we all look out for one another. Wouldn't that be a beautiful place to live in?

We aren't after a future that will, ultimately, not exist, where everything is dried up, used, dead, and consumed. We don't want that for our future generations. No one wants the world to fade away. And that's the beauty in it! In all these people coming together, loving every second of living greener, because we all share a common goal.

We have a chance, but not time to think too long about it. The world, whether we like it or not, will go on without us and even forget us, if it has to. So, I hope you decide to join the eco-life and hug as many trees as you wish and scream, "Go Green!"

And then the world flocked together to join the murmuration unfolding in the sky. We're all up here. Tell me, do you see it?

* * *

I would like to thank you, reader, not only for reading and listening to what I have to say but for sticking through every bit and piece, even through my dad jokes! And yes, even though they were probably just as bad as all of these problems, our environment is no laughing matter. This is our home and we have to look after it as it has done for us. But also, remember that change doesn't have to be so heavy and intense. We could still tackle all of these problems and do our part with our humor intact, a smile on our faces, and a confident, optimistic stance. And besides, helping our planet is much more fun when you let your hair down! But I do hope I made you smile and I'll leave you with one more.

A climate denier and a climate change scientist walks into a bar. The denier says, "Nice to see you." The climate scientist says, "Nice to CO_2."

Not that *that's* out of my system, you know what to do. I've given you enough to give it a running start, and always refresh your knowledge, look at more crafts, new inventions, tips, tricks, and hacks. They're all over the place! So, what do you say? Let's change the world one step at a time, together! And please leave a comment, so we could have more people over on the green side!

A SPECIAL GIFT FOR MY READERS

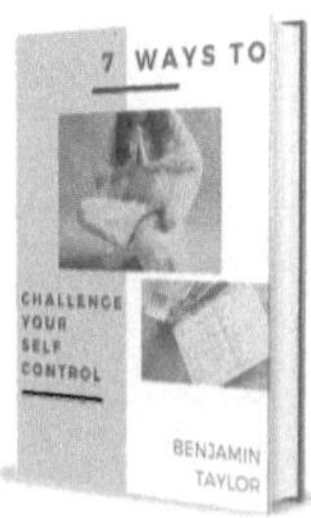

Included with your purchase of this book is our
Bonus Content,

7 Ways to Challenge Your Self-Control.

This booklet is a training for you to try with small day-to-day habits before you move on to making big changes in your life. These mini challenges can help you improve your health, and can help you save more money!

Click the link below and let us know which email address to deliver to
https://benjamintaylor.activehosted.com/f/1

REFERENCES

6 strategies to improve living standards. (2021, April 30). Tutor2u. https://www.tutor2u.net/economics/reference/6-strategies-to-improve-living-standards

10 ways to create an eco friendly home. (n.d.). Lowes. Retrieved October 31, 2021, https://www.lowes.ca/ideas-how-to/inspiration/ways-to-create-an-eco-friendly-home

12 small changes to make your home more eco-friendly. (2020, May 12). Biofriendly Planet for a Cooler Environment. https://biofriendlyplanet.com/eco-friendly-tips/12-small-changes-to-make-your-home-more-eco-friendly/

21 good reasons to go green. (2017, December 24). Conserve Energy Future. https://www.conserve-energy-future.com/21-good-reasons-to-go-green.php

50 creative ways to repurpose, reuse and upcycle old things. (2012, June 12). TwistedSifter. https://twistedsifter.com/2012/06/creative-ways-to-repurpose-reuse-and-upcycle-old-things/

Aguirre, S. (2021, April 22). *Learn how to start eco-friendly cleaning in your home.* The Spruce. https://www.thespruce.com/what-is-green-cleaning-1900463

All Green. (2020, April 3). *Types of recycling.* All Green Electronics Recycling. https://allgreenrecycling.com/types-of-recycling/

Anisha. (2017, April 26). *5 countries that have revolutionised the way they tackle waste.* NDTV-Dettol Banega Swasth Swachh India.   https://swachhindia.ndtv.com/5-countries-revolutionised-way-tackle-trash-waste-5013/

Ashley. (2014, June 30). *How to reuse 13 things you would normally throw away.* My Heart Beets. https://myheartbeets.com/reuse-13-things-normally-throw-away/

Barnard, H. (2019, November 21). *What's the best way to improve living standards?* JRF. https://www.jrf.org.uk/blog/whats-best-way-improve-living-standards

BBC News. (2020, April 29). Wild animals enjoy freedom of a quieter world. BBC News. www.bbc.com/news/world-52459487

Berrill, A., Card, N., Cable, J., Harper, L., Blanchard, T., Hughes, S., & Ferguson, D. (2020, February 29). 50 simple ways to make your life greener. *The Guardian,* www.theguardian.com/environment/2020/feb/29/50-ways-to-green-up-your-life-save-the-planet

Bogle, J. (2020, June 26). *The 14 countries doing the most to protect the environment.* Reader's Digest. https://www.rd.com/list/countries-doing-the-most-to-protect-the-environment/

Brigida, A.-C. (2018, May 7). *From Australia to El Salvador to Vietnam, the environment is finally getting its day in court.* Down to Earth. https://www.downtoearth.org.in/news/environment/from-australia-to-el-salvador-to-vietnam-the-environment-is-finally-getting-its-day-in-court-60437

Bumpus. (n.d.). *Light bulb lamp.* Instructables Workshop. www.instructables.com/Light-Bulb-Lamp/

Cammers in Workshop. (2012). *Coat hooks from cheap spoons.* Instructables. https://www.instructables.com/Coat-Hooks-from-Cheap-Spoons/

Circle of Blue. (2018, October 5). *Experts name the top 19 solutions to the global freshwater crisis.* Circle of Blue. https://www.circleofblue.org/2010/world/experts-name-the-top-19-solutions-to-the-global-freshwater-crisis/

Deutsche Welle (2019). *Five of the world's biggest environmental problems.* Deutsche Welle. https://www.dw.com/en/five-of-the-worlds-biggest-environmental-problems/a-35915705

de Souza, K. (2020, July 21). *Chief Seattle: 'We do not inherit the Earth from our ancestors.'* karenadesouza.com/seattle-we-do-not-inherit-the-earth-from-our-ancestors/#:~:text=21%20Jul%20Chief%20Seattle%3A%20

DIY: Mini notebook from a cereal box. (2021). Creme de La Carte. http://www.cremedelacraft.com/2012/06/diy-mini-notebook-from-cereal-box.html

Double Glazing Network. (n.d.). *Average double glazing prices.* Double Glazing Network. Retrieved October 31, 2021, https://www.doubleglazingnetwork.com/double-glazing-cost/

Ellie, K. (2019). *7 Tips on how to thrift shop like a boss.* The Good Trade. https://www.thegoodtrade.com/features/thrift-shopping-tips

EnergySage. (2019). *2019 pros and cons of electric cars.* Energysage. https://www.energysage.com/electric-vehicles/101/pros-and-cons-electric-cars/

Environmental Protection. (2016). *Tips: Top ten ways to recycle.* Environmental Protection. https://eponline.com/articles/2007/11/12/tips-top-ten-ways-to-recycle.aspx

Fleming, S. (2020, January 3). *The war on plastic: 5 green laws for 2020.* World Economic Forum. https://www.weforum.org/agenda/2020/01/green-laws-environment-2020/

Geller, L. (2020, August 18). *You couldn't kill these indoor plants if you tried.* Women's Health. https://www.womenshealthmag.com/life/g26610281/best-indoor-plants/

Gifford, D. (2017, April 8). *100 things you can (and should) compost.* Small Footprint Family. https://www.smallfootprintfamily.com/100-things-you-can-compost

Goodwill. (2020, May 14). *What does it mean to go thrifting?* Goodwill of Central and Northern Arizona. https://www.goodwillaz.org/what-does-it-mean-to-go-thrifting-2/

Goodwill Ohio Valley. (2020, February 24). *5 incredible benefits of thrift shopping.* Goodwill Cincinnati. https://www.cincinnatigoodwill.org/benefits-of-thrift-shopping/

Gray, R. (2017). *The biggest energy challenges facing humanity.* BBC Future. https://www.bbc.com/future/article/20170313-the-biggest-energy-challenges-facing-humanity

Green America. (n.d.). *10 habits of highly sustainable people.* (n.d.) Green America. Retrieved October 31, 2021, https://www.greenamerica.org/green-living/10-habits-highly-sustainable-people

Green America. (n.d.). *First steps to efficiency*. Green America. Retrieved October 10, 2021, https://www.greenamerica.org/first-steps-efficiency

Green Mountain Energy. (2017). *Ways you can protect the environment*. Green Mountain Energy Company. https://www.greenmountainenergy.com/why-renewable-energy/protect-the-environment/

Greene, E. (n.d.). *Eco-travel checklist*. Green America. Retrieved October 31, 2021, https://www.greenamerica.org/green-living/eco-travel-checklist

Greentumble. (2016, August 1). *Countries with the most sophisticated waste management*. Greentumble. https://greentumble.com/countries-with-the-most-sophisticated-waste-management/

Healthline. (2020, March 30). *Here's why you can't break that bad habit*. Healthline. https://www.healthline.com/health/how-long-does-it-take-to-break-a-habit#tips-and-tricks

Just Energy. (n.d.). *The top 9 environmental problems*. Just Energy. Retrieved October 31, 2021, https://justenergy.com/blog/the-top-9-environmental-problems/

Koh, A., & Ragu, A. (2020). *Are you a robot?* Bloomberg. https://www.bloomberg.com/news/features/2019-07-11/how-the-world-can-solve-its-2-billion-ton-trash-problem

Kristyna. (2018, April 16). *8 reasons to buy second hand items*. LazyFrugal. https://lazyfrugal.com/8-reasons-to-buy-second-hand-items/

McCloy, J. (2018, September 4). *Advantages of going green: Help the environment.* Greencoast. https://green-coast.org/advantages-of-going-green-help-the-environment

McCulloch, N. (2019, September 3). *What can I recycle: A guide to what makes something recyclable.* Rubicon: Software Company Offering Smart Waste and Recycling Solutions. https://www.rubicon.com/blog/what-can-be-recycled/

Morse, I. (2021, May 20). *Millions of electric cars are coming. What happens to all the dead batteries?* Science. www.science.org/content/article/millions-electric-cars-are-coming-what-happens-all-dead-batteries

Moreau, K. (2014, June 23). *DIY a suitcase table in 3 easy steps.* Good Housekeeping. https://www.goodhousekeeping.com/home/craft-ideas/how-to/g1161/suitcase-table/?slide=4

Most environmentally friendly countries 2020. (2021). World Population Review. https://worldpopulationreview.com/country-rankings/most-environmentally-friendly-countries

Murray, J. (2020, March 9). *Eight of the top vertical farming companies in the world.* NS Agriculture. https://www.nsagriculture.com/news/vertical-farming-companies/

My Mommy Style, and Camille. (2015, June 20). *50 easy DIY projects made from items in your recycling bin.* My Mommy Style. www.mymommystyle.com/50-easy-diy-projects-made-from-items-in-your-recycling-bin/

National Geographic. (2019, January 14). *Global warming effects.* National Geographic. https://www.nationalgeographic.com/environment/article/global-warming-effects

Netflix. (2019, March 19) *Our Planet.* [Video] YouTube. Retrieved October 26, 2021, www.youtube.com/watch?v=aETNYyrqNYE

Noll, M. (2019, February 29). All about indoor composting. *Better Homes & Gardens.* https://www.bhg.com/gardening/yard/compost/diy-indoor-compost-bin

NPR Staff. (2011, December 9). *What countries are doing to tackle climate change.* NPR. https://www.npr.org/2011/12/07/143302823/what-countries-are-doing-to-tackle-climate-change

OpenMind. (2020, February 10). *5 recycling lessons from different countries in the world.* OpenMind. https://www.bbvaopenmind.com/en/science/environment/5-recycling-lessons-from-different-countries-in-the-world/

Parker, T. (2019, March 18). *World recycling day: Here's the five best recycling countries in the world.* NS Packaging. https://www.nspackaging.com/analysis/best-recycling-countries/

Paskill, A. (2020, April 8). *8 simple ways to help the environment.* Fastweb. https://www.fastweb.com/student-life/articles/eight-simple-ways-to-help-the-environment

PlanetNatural. (2019). *What to compost.* Planet Natural. https://www.planetnatural.com/composting-101/making/what-to-use

Real Life Options. (2016, May 12). *Go green in 10 simple steps.* Real Life Options. https://reallifeoptions.org/go-green-in-10-simple-steps/

Recycling jokes. (n.d.). Upjokes. https://upjoke.com/recycling-jokes

Richardson, L. (2018, October 14). *The advantages and disadvantages of solar energy: 10 pros and cons.* EnergySage. https://news.energysage.com/advantages-and-disadvantages-of-solar-energy/

Rinkesh. (n.d.). *41+ best environmental jokes of all time that will make you laugh.* Conserve Energy Future. Retrieved October 31, 2021, https://www.conserve-energy-future.com/best-environmental-jokes.php

Rinkesh. (2016, December 25). *What are top 25 environmental concerns?* Conserve Energy Future. https://www.conserve-energy-future.com/top-25-environmental-concerns.php

Salkeld, A. (n.d.). *The 7 best flowers for honeybees.* Buddha Bee Apiary. Retrieved October 31, 2021, https://www.buddhabeeapiary.com/blog/what-flowers-do-honeybees-like

Seasongoods, S. (2014, December 1). *Easy home office organization ideas.* Hometalk. https://www.hometalk.com/diy/organize/command-centers-boards/turn-a-cookie-sheet-into-a-magnetic-memo-board-5979699

Sharma, A. (2014, January 31). *Habit formation: Basis, types and measures for effective habit formation.* Psychology Discussion. https://www.psychologydiscussion.net/habits/habit-formation-basis-types-and-measures-for-effective-habit-formation/638

Shulkosky, M. (2012, June 23). *10 reasons we should all shop at thrift stores.* ToughNickel. https://toughnickel.com/frugal-living/X-Reasons-We-Should-All-Shop-at-Thrift-Shops

Sloop, S., Crandon, L., Allen, M., Koetje, K., Reed, L., Gaines, L., Sirisaksoontorn, W., & Lerner, M. (2020, September 25). *A direct recycling case study from a lithium-ion battery recall.*

Sustainable Materials and Technologies. https://doi.org/10.1016/j.susmat.2020.e00152

Smith, M. (2017, January 20). *How to make a mirror out of a tennis racket—8 steps.* Onehowto.com, 20 Jan. 2017, home.onehowto.com/article/how-to-make-a-mirror-out-of-a-tennis-racket-5637.html

Statista Research Department. (2021, September 28) *Countries with most murder cases.* Statista. Retrieved October 30, 2021, www.statista.com/statistics/262963/ranking-the-20-countries-with-the-most-murders-per-100-000-inhabitants/

Stebbins, S. (2019, July 14). Countries doing the most (and least) to protect the environment. *USA Today.* https://www.usatoday.com/story/money/2019/07/14/climate-change-countries-doing-most-least-to-protect-environment/39534413/

susan1882. (2020, September 17). *Five key steps of recycling for growing the circular economy.* Recycling Connections. https://www.recyclingconnections.org/post/five-steps-of-recycling

Thadani, A. (2019, December 20). *What is green cleaning (and why should you care)?* ThreeMain. https://www.threemain.com/blogs/education/what-is-green-cleaning-and-why-should-you-care

The 16+ best pollution jokes. (n.d.). Upjoke. Retrieved October 31, 2021, https://upjoke.com/pollution-jokes

Thompson, C (2021, June 7). *What can you do with used clothing not suitable for donation?* KQED. www.kqed.org/news/11491076/what-can-you-do-with-used-clothing-not-suitable-for-donation

U.S. Department of Energy. (2019). *Alternative fuels data center: Electric vcehicle benefits and considerations.* https://afdc.energy.gov/fuels/electricity_benefits.html

United Nations. (2019, February 19). *Raising living standards boosts overall well-being of societies, speakers say, as commission for social development continues session.* https://www.un.org/press/en/2019/soc4875.doc.htm

United Nations Climate Change. (2018). *Katowice Climate Change Conference, December 2018.* UNFCC. https://unfcc-c.int/process-and-meetings/conferences/katowice-climate-change-conference-december-2018/katowice-climate-change-conference-december-2018

University of Toronto. (2011, October 11). *How to identify truly green products.* Treehugger. https://www.treehugger.com/how-identify-truly-green-products-4857536

US EPA. (2018a, August 1). *Recycling basics.* US Environmental Protection Agency. https://www.epa.gov/recycle/recycling-basics

US EPA. (2018b, November 27). *Local renewable energy benefits and resources.* US Environmental Protection Agency. https://www.epa.gov/statelocalenergy/local-renewable-energy-benefits-and-resources

Weiss-Roessler, J. (2014, June 24). *20 amazing benefits of thrift shopping you probably never expected.* Lifehack. https://www.lifehack.org/articles/lifestyle/20-amazing-benefits-thrift-shopping-you-probably-never-expected.html

World Bank. (n.d.). *Trends in solid waste management.* World Bank. Retrieved October 31, 2021, https://datatopics.worldbank.org/what-a-waste/trends_in_solid_waste_management.html#:~:text=The%20world%20generates%202.01%20billion

World Wildlife Fund. (2021). *Water scarcity*. World Wildlife Fund. https://www.worldwildlife.org/threats/water-scarcity

Zuckerman, A. (2020, May 11). *60 recycling statistics: 2020/2021 data trends and predictions.* CompareCamp. comparecamp.com/recycling-statistics/